FAMOUS HUMANITARIANS

FAMOUS HUMANITARIANS

by

WILLIAM OLIVER STEVENS

Illustrated

DODD, MEAD & COMPANY
NEW YORK   1953

J
923.6
S

35069

To

My Sister,

Maria Elizabeth Phenix

INTRODUCTION

THE LONG RISE of mankind from the jungle to civilization owes much to the unselfish men and women whose lives, like bright stars, have shown the path upward. These noble spirits we call humanitarians, because their lives were dedicated to humanity, to bringing help, kindness and consideration to the suffering and the unfortunate. Scientists have made great contributions, and so have explorers and inventors, but it is the humanitarian who has brought about the greatest difference between barbarism and civilization. This difference has two main principles, closely related to each other. They are respect for human life and help for the suffering.

In the great civilizations of the past, these principles were practically unknown. In Greece, especially in Sparta, a baby who was born crippled or who merely looked like a weakling, was tossed out on a hillside, to die of exposure or to be eaten by wolves. In Roman history the noblest characters were the Stoics; yet in their philosophy, also, human life was cheap and pity was only a contemptible sign of weakness.

The change to our modern standards has been slow, but it was largely brought about by the Judaic-Christian Bible and the religions that sprang from these scriptures. Even today the contrast between the traditions of the peoples that have had the Bible and those who have not can be seen, not only in the cruel practices of savages in the jungle, but also among nations that have developed an ancient civilization of their own. For example, until the British put a stop to these practices, Hindu mothers tossed their unwelcome girl babies to the crocodiles, and Hindu widows were expected to fling themselves into the flames on the funeral pyres of their husbands.

China shows a similar picture. In a recent book *Brain Surgeon* by Dr.

Introduction

William Sharpe, the author tells of a Chinese father who, in his village square, publicly beheaded what he called a good-for-nothing son. According to Chinese standards, this act saved the honor of the family, because if the boy had been arrested by the police, as was likely, the family would have lost face forever. In China, too, superfluous girl babies were sold into slavery.

As to respect for human life in itself, the same author tells of how he once came upon a small group of Chinese peering over a wall on a river front. It turned out that ten feet from that wall a man was struggling in the water. The onlookers were laughing and betting on how soon he would go under for the last time. Dr. Sharpe jumped into the water, pulled the man to the wharf and gave him first aid. At this the bettors were furious because, they said, he had spoiled their fun. And they snarled that the River Spirit would get him because he had saved the man from drowning!

This contempt for the life of others has always been part of the Asiatic tradition. The present writer, as a small boy in Burma, once saw a native fishing boat overturn in the swollen waters of the Irrawaddy River. There were other boats, with their crews, pulled up along the river bank, but not one put out to rescue the two men of the overturned boat, who were struggling in the middle of the wide river. The idea was, "Why should we bother? Suppose they do drown, what of it?" And the two men did drown. Nobody cared except their families.

Another cruel tradition with a long history has been that cripples and the insane are funny. Homer, for instance, tells of a banquet of the gods on Mount Olympus. When the lame god Hephaistos came limping into the banquet hall, the poet says "inextinguishable laughter" arose around the table. And in spite of Bible teachings, this idea persisted many centuries in Christian Europe. A king's jester was often a hunchback, because that deformity was something to laugh at. Even today there are people who think that a half-wit is funny. On our modern stage, too, a drunken person is considered a comic character. Some day our descendants will wonder how we could think drunkenness amusing.

In this book only twenty humanitarians are presented, and some very briefly. Of course, there have been many, many more, some of them perhaps

Introduction

equally deserving of mention and equally famous. Countless other men and women have been just as devoted and unselfish, but were never known to fame outside their own communities because their lives never attracted public notice: priests, ministers, missionaries, Sisters of Charity, doctors, nurses and countless other unselfish souls in everyday walks of life. These all gave unstintingly of their time, their means and their strength in helping the unfortunate. We call these people humanitarians rather than philanthropists, because the latter are the kindly men of wealth who give their money to good causes, while the former give their whole lives. This book tells about some of these humanitarians, men and women, who gave their all to bettering the lot of those who suffer.

W.O.S.

CONTENTS

SAINT VINCENT DE PAUL

SAINT VINCENT DE PAUL

I. SAINT VINCENT DE PAUL

April 24, 1581—September 27, 1660

USUALLY, when a French name has a "de" in front of it, we think of the family as belonging to the aristocracy, as Marquis de Lafayette. But in the village of Pouy, in which Saint Vincent de Paul was born, everybody used a "de" just to make it easy to identify themselves with their homes and their families. Saint Vincent always wrote his own name "Depaul," so that no one would think that he was putting on airs, and he referred to himself throughout his life simply as "Monsieur Vincent." This was the title given to a French film story of his life which was shown in America a few years ago.

The boy Vincent was kept busy tending his father's livestock, especially the sheep. The father must have been a man of unusual vision for a simple peasant, because he soon realized that his boy had a mind that deserved an education. Of course, in that day there were no public schools anywhere, and sending the lad to school meant paying out money. But that is just what this wise father did, even though it must have meant a real sacrifice.

Not only did Vincent make good at school, but he did so well that his father planned for him the one career then open for a peasant boy with brains; that is, the priesthood. This meant going to the university, with still more expense, but the father promptly sold a yoke of oxen for the entrance fee, and off the young man went to the University of Toulouse. As might be expected, Vincent did all he could to work his way through. Again he made a brilliant record, and was ordained a priest at the unusual age of eighteen.

This event took place in the year 1600. To relate that year to American history, we may remember that it was seven years before Captain John Smith

3

and his followers landed at Jamestown, and twenty years before the Pilgrims set foot on Plymouth Rock.

It was not long afterward that the young priest had an important errand in the city of Narbonne, and since it was cheaper to travel by sea than by land, he boarded a vessel. In those days all journeys on the Mediterranean were risky, because the Moors on the north shore of Africa, called the Barbary Coast, made piracy their big business. Their victims were the merchant ships of Christian nations, and all the passengers and crews whom they took alive they sold into slavery. In Saint Vincent's time, it is estimated that there were between 25,000 and 30,000 Christian slaves treated like beasts of burden in these North African cities.

At the time, the Christian nations were so jealous of one another that they did nothing to stop this piracy. Instead, they sank to the level of paying yearly tribute to buy the brigands off. Even as late as the early nineteenth century, Great Britain was paying the pirates to spare British ships, but they could do what they liked to the others. The first determined stroke to end all this was delivered by the little American navy in 1801, when a squadron attacked the city of Tripoli, then the worst of the pirate cities. But in Saint Vincent's day the Barbary pirates did as they pleased.

It happened that the ship with the young priest on board was captured by a pirate from Tunis. Several of the passengers were killed or wounded in the encounter, Saint Vincent being among the latter, though not seriously. After landing in Tunis he had all his clothes taken away from him and, dressed only in a pair of linen drawers, he was paraded through the streets, with the other victims, in order to attract buyers. On the auction block he was bought by a fisherman; but, to the master's disgust, he soon found out that his new Christian slave was so constantly seasick that he was useless in the fishing business. Here was a case where seasickness proved to be a blessing in disguise. If Saint Vincent had been a hardy seaman, he would no doubt have spent all the rest of his life in slavery.

He then became the slave of two other masters. The second of these was a man from the province of Savoy, in southeastern France, formerly a Franciscan friar, who had turned Mohammedan and was living with a harem of three wives. The Christian slave so worked on his master that he brought him to his knees in remorse. Finally, taking the priest with him, he went back to his native land. In this way Saint Vincent escaped, but during the rest of his life he never forgot the miserable lot of the Christian slaves in the Barbary states.

A few years later he was appointed tutor-priest in the family of a nobleman, Philippe de Gondi, who held the office of General of the Galleys. His two sons were the pupils, and a lady who knew them described them as "two demons," a pair of spoiled brats who made life as unpleasant as possible for their instructor. But his patron's office brought Saint Vincent into contact with the galleys, and there he saw human wretchedness even worse than anything he had witnessed at Tunis.

These galleys were a part of the French navy. They were open-decked vessels, lateen-rigged (triangular sails), but dependent almost entirely on oars. The officers were quartered aft. Down the middle ran a platform or deck, on either side of which ranged the benches for the rowers, open to the weather. To be sentenced to the galleys was a punishment reserved for only the most hardened criminals who had escaped hanging. These wretches were no better off than the galley slaves of ancient Rome. Each had a heavy cannon ball chained to his leg. Sometimes they were forced to row for twenty-four hours without rest. If one collapsed he was thrown overboard, cannon ball and all. As can be imagined, the death rate was fearful. The overseer walked back and forth on the middle deck, cracking his whip on their bare backs when he wasn't setting the stroke.

The most familiar story about Saint Vincent is that once he allowed a galley convict to escape in order to rejoin his wife and children, and took his place for a while on the rowers' bench. This story is told in different ways; one version was played up in a dramatic scene in the moving picture. But later scholarship has proved that it is only a legend. What Saint Vincent did do for these unhappy creatures was not so theatrical but much more important. He made them believe that he was interested in them personally, and worked to better their hard fate as far as he could. They had never known anyone else like that. And he brought many of them back to the one consolation even a galley‧slave could have, his religion. That he succeeded among so many of these hardened criminals whose hearts were full of hatred and thirst for vengeance is a miracle in itself.

The next period of his life is studded with many charitable works. Before going to the De Gondi family, he had been a member of the household of the Princess Marguerite de Valois, and while at the De Gondis also he met many men and women of the aristocracy. It would have been the easiest thing in the world for him to accept the post of chaplain in the family of some nobleman and live a life of ease, with a fine library to enjoy, and only a light program of priestly duties. But that was not the nature of this man. He felt a call to help the friendless, the poor, the outcast. He kept his contacts with his friends of the aristocracy because he needed their wealth and their influence to make his charitable plans come true, but for himself it was a life consecrated to the unhappy. He had known the despair of the Christian slaves in Tunis; he had seen the even more dreadful life of the convicts pulling the oars in the galleys. Memories of his own boyhood then led him to look into the conditions of the peasants on the De Gondi estates.

Here he found a different kind of need. He discovered that the local clergy were lax in their duties toward these people. In one parish he found a family in sore need. He preached a sermon about them the next Sunday. At once a dozen kind women went to the cottage with baskets of food, and soon others offered to help in needy cases, too. At this show of fine spirit, he called together everyone interested and founded the first known charity organization in France. The peasants would come to him to tell of their needs, and the more prosperous women would send baskets of food or clothing for distribution to them. To the rich and aristocratic ladies Saint Vincent went, saying "Give me of your jewels." And they did. Madame de Gondi was so delighted that she gave a handsome sum of money to put the organization on a sound footing financially. Out of this simple beginning have grown all the countless Saint Vincent de Paul societies in the world today.

Then he bent his steps toward the Paris slums, and there he found so many kinds of misery and degradation that he could not rest until he had done something about it. Nobody else in France seemed to care whether these slum-dwellers lived or died. For one thing, he discovered that a great many unwanted babies perished of neglect. Here was a cause that he knew would appeal to the women, and he went to work. Before long he had established the Foundlings Hospital, where unhappy mothers could bring their babies and know that they would be cared for. The Foundlings Hospital now in Paris stands as one of the many monuments to Saint Vincent de Paul.

One day, as Saint Vincent walked the streets of Paris, he saw a beggar beating a child. When the priest demanded an explanation, the scoundrel said frankly that a crying child was more likely to attract pity and a copper coin. Investigating further, Saint Vincent discovered that in the slums there was a school for beggars, to teach them all the tricks of that trade, and that little children were the sufferers. It was taught there that a beggar's child must be crying and look thin and starved. If the little ones were blind or covered with sores or crippled, they made all the better bait for pity; and it can easily be imagined what happened to the children hired by the professional beggars for their "racket."

There were so many other evil practices as well as so much innocent suffering, especially among the children, the old and the sick, that the good priest was appalled. He told his story so movingly to the fine ladies and gentlemen of his acquaintance that they gave generously, and he founded another society for the city of Paris, "The Fraternity of Charity."

But he realized that charitable work needed persons who would give their whole lives, not just money. So, backed by another wealthy lady, Mademoiselle de Gras, he organized a "Daughters of Charity." For the men he was able to obtain the use of an old palace called Saint Lazare, to be turned into a training school for the workers. The women who were Daughters of Charity wore a simple gray uniform, so as to be easily recognized. The men who graduated from St. Lazare were sent out into the villages, two by two, for deeds of practical kindness. Both the men and the women of these organizations were held to a strict discipline, and no volunteer was accepted without first passing a testing period. Saint Vincent kept a watchful eye on them and demanded a high standard of self-devotion.

But in the midst of his great work for humanity there came disaster, the five darkest years of his life. This was a period of civil war, known in history as "The Fronde," which lasted from 1648 to 1653. It grew out of a revolt against the men who were ruling France during the childhood of Louis XIV and who had stolen away all the rights the people ever had. And, to make matters worse, religion was an issue, Protestants and Catholics. In this fighting the peasants suffered terribly. Their crops were trampled and their houses destroyed. Saint Vincent collected seeds for the farmers and set up soup kitchens for the starving. But all that he could do was little against the widespread misery. A famine set in, and the people gnawed wood, ate rats and made soup out of boiled leather. Then, when Paris was shut off from food supplies, the famine reached the city. Royalty and the court nobility fled, turning a deaf ear to Saint Vincent's pleas for those who couldn't run away. The most cruel blow to his heart came when someone spread the lying rumor that the priest also had fled. Then a mob, furious at being deserted by their one friend, stormed St. Lazare and in one hour destroyed his work of many years.

Space does not permit the full story here of what this wonderful man did to reform the Paris prisons; of the missionaries he sent to the Christian slaves of the Barbary coast, with agents to arrange ransoms; the neglected little ones and the old and helpless whom he rescued; and, during the civil war, the wounded soldiers that he saved who had been left lying on the ground to die. How one man had the strength, the time and the organizing ability to accomplish all these deeds of Christian kindness is hard to understand. But he relied on a strength above his own. He was a man of prayer and unshakable faith. To him, nothing attempted in the name of God was impossible.

In 1658 he was in a carriage collision and was thrown so violently to the ground that for a long time his life was despaired of. He made a partial recovery, but it was followed by a painful invalidism as a result of that accident. Unfortunately, the physicians of that day knew so little that they only increased his pain and hastened his death. On September 27, 1660, the long ordeal of suffering ended.

All who knew Saint Vincent testified to his deep humility and utter lack of selfishness. For all his achievements in behalf of the miserable and destitute, he never received any high Church office. To the end he was officially just a priest; to himself only "Monsieur Vincent." But to the world then and now he became one of the truest saints. He was canonized in 1737, long after that noble life had ended.

There are today in the United States many Saint Vincent Hospitals, keeping alive his memory in a land that he never saw. And there are many other organizations, religious and charitable, which also had their origin in his warm heart. Perhaps no more fitting title can be given to Saint Vincent than that used in one of the best biographies we have of him in English, "The Apostle of Charity."

EDWARD JENNER
WALTER REED

EDWARD JENNER

WALTER REED

II. EDWARD JENNER

May 17, 1749—January 26, 1823

WALTER REED

September 13, 1851—November 22, 1902

THE TWO MEN named above are included among the world's famous humanitarians because they devoted their lives to conquering certain terrible diseases that had plagued mankind for centuries. Edward Jenner was the English doctor who discovered how to prevent smallpox. This dread disease, like leprosy, had been known from earliest times, but it was not formally described until an Arab physician wrote about it in the ninth century. Also, like leprosy, smallpox was spread over Europe by soldiers returning from the Crusades. It reached and ravaged England during the thirteenth century.

In the New World smallpox was unknown until the arrival of the Spanish explorers. Early in the sixteenth century they brought it to Santo Domingo and then to Mexico, where it is said to have killed three million people. It proved especially fatal to primitive peoples, such as the native Indians and the Negro slaves. But it was the ever-present terror of all civilized peoples, too. And it reached into the homes of the wealthy and high-born, as well as into the hovels of the poor and lowly.

It was not only the threat of death that it brought to its victims, but, in a large proportion of cases, permanent injury to those that survived. Many were left crippled or totally blind. And everyone who recovered carried on

his face pockmarks, sometimes so many and so deep as to make one dis-
figured for life. Many a beautiful belle recovered from smallpox so badly
pock-marked that she shunned society thereafter and covered her face with a
veil when she went out.

How many died every year in Europe and America from this plague no
one can tell, but no preventive had been discovered until an English doctor
named Edward Jenner devoted his life to finding an answer to the smallpox
problem, and succeeded. Jenner was the son of a country vicar in a small
town named Berkeley, in Gloucestershire, England. He learned the science
of medicine, after the fashion of the eighteenth century, by being apprenticed
to a surgeon. After that, in the year 1770, he became a sort of resident student
in the home of a famous London doctor, John Hunter. This man inspired
young Edward with the spirit of scientific discovery in the field of healing.
From Dr. Hunter, Jenner went to the Saint George Hospital for more study,
and then, by 1773, he was back in his native town of Berkeley. There he made
his home with his older brother and began his practice.

From the first, the young physician made a name for himself. He distinguished himself by the care with which he dressed when he rode out to call
on his patients, for he wore a bright blue coat and high top boots with silver
spurs, an unusual costume for a country doctor. But far more important was
the success that he had in his medical practice. In his spare time he enjoyed
many hobbies, for he played the flute and the violin, studied birds and flowers,
and even wrote verse.

How he found any time for hobbies is a mystery, for when he married, in
the year 1788, his practice was so large that he had to give up surgery in
order to devote all his energies to medicine. Though only a country doctor,
his name spread far beyond his village and county. He was the first to show
that a certain disease of the heart, called angina, was due to the hardening
of the arteries, and that the heart played an important part in certain types
of rheumatism. In 1792, Jenner was awarded the honorary degree of Doctor
of Medicine by the University of St. Andrews in Scotland.

All the while, he was becoming more deeply interested in smallpox than
in any other phase of medicine. Country folk told him that any dairymaid

Edward Jenner

who had had cowpox was safe against smallpox. Cowpox and swine pox were related diseases of animals which could be communicated to humans. If it were true that a person who had had cowpox—a mild disease—was thereby protected from smallpox, a terrible disease, why not make use of it? Jenner brooded over this idea for many years, but waited a long time before putting it to the test. He could not try it on himself because he was already immune, but he could try it on his son. This was done only after much prayerful consideration by both parents, and when Jenner was very sure that he was right. He inoculated the child with swine pox. Little Eddie was mildly sick with this, but when his father injected him with smallpox, he resisted it completely. Then and there, with his own boy, Jenner had proved his discovery.

On May 14, 1796, he made a public demonstration by injecting into the arms of an eight-year-old boy, James Phipps, who had had cowpox virus and had recovered quickly, the virus of smallpox, with no bad effects. Jenner then went to London to spread his discovery, but to his dismay he was at first bitterly attacked by both doctors and clergymen. Yet, strange to say, it took only about one year to win that battle. Therefore, practically all the leaders in medical circles begged him to move to London to teach them how this new preventive miracle was done. St. Thomas's Hospital offered him the huge sum, for those days, of ten thousand pounds if he would settle in London. But he declined and went back to his country town in order to give all his time to vaccinating there among the rural people and to preparing pure lymph to send out to other doctors to use. In following this program he had to give up all his personal practice and soon had nothing to live on, except a small income he had inherited. But his success was so striking that his friends successfully petitioned Parliament for a money grant of ten thousand pounds in 1802, and another sum of twenty thousand pounds five years later. In 1803 he founded the Royal Institute to combat smallpox.

When he made his public demonstration on Jimmy Phipps, he took the vaccine virus from the skin of a milkmaid who had contracted cowpox. (The word "vaccine" comes from the Latin word *vacca* meaning cow.) In this story of the conquest of smallpox it is only fair to give second place of honor to an Italian doctor, Luigi Sacco, of Milan, who devoted his life to this cause and succeeded in bringing about the use of virus taken from animals, cows and horses, rather than human beings. And that is the way it has been done ever since.

From England the fame of Edward Jenner's discovery spread all over Europe and America. In Russia, where the pestilence used to kill as many as two million people in a single year, the Empress showed her gratitude to Dr. Jenner by sending him a diamond ring; and the first Russian child vaccinated she named "Vaccinoff," and had him pensioned for life! Honors and gifts poured in on Dr. Jenner from Asia, too, where smallpox had been even more deadly than in Russia. A gold medal was sent him by the surgeons in the British navy in token of their gratitude for the lives saved in the armed forces by vaccination.

In America a terrible blunder was made at first in introducing vaccination, because smallpox pustules were used instead of cowpox, an error which, of course, only spread the plague. But that was soon corrected. And among the gifts that Edward Jenner received from this side of the Atlantic was a belt of wampum from a tribe of American Indians. The best tribute in words was sent by President Jefferson: "You have erased from the calendar of human affliction one of its greatest. . . Mankind can never forget that you lived."

It was in his native town of Berkeley that Jenner died—loved, honored and venerated by his townsfolk for his generous services to them. He cared nothing for making money; he could easily have made a fortune from his discovery, but instead he tossed away his own practice so that the hundreds of country folk who thronged in front of his door might receive, without cost from his hands, their protection against smallpox. Fortunately, he lived to see his discovery recognized by the medical profession all over the world. One noted physician expressed the thought of the entire profession when he spoke of vaccination as "the greatest discovery ever made in medicine."

Walter Reed

This other doctor who discovered the cause and prevention of a great and deadly plague, Walter Reed, was born almost exactly one hundred years after Edward Jenner. By a coincidence, his native county in Virginia bore the same name as Jenner's, "Gloucester." While smallpox was an ancient Old World disease brought to the American colonies by the white men, the pestilence which Reed overcame was peculiar to the New World, especially the Southern Hemisphere. The only other part of the world where it took a foothold was on the western coast of Africa, and it is possible that it was brought there by slave ships from the West Indies. Those islands, together with coasts of Central and South America, seemed to be the special breeding place for one of the most fatal diseases known to man, yellow fever.

Although this plague was commonly found only in warm-weather areas, early in the nineteenth century it also ravaged Philadelphia and New York. In the mid-nineteenth century it almost depopulated the city of Norfolk, Virginia. But the worst area was always the Caribbean. In 1819 Commodore Oliver Hazard Perry, hero of the Battle of Lake Erie, was sent on a mission to Venezuela to put an end by negotiation to the piracy backed by Venezuelan officials. He died of yellow fever contracted while he was in a town on the Orinoco river. Shortly afterwards a flotilla under another naval hero of the War of 1812, David Porter, was dispatched to the West Indies to fight the pirates who were attacking American shipping in those waters. The Americans soon discovered that yellow fever was a far greater danger than pirates. Porter himself fell a victim and nearly died. Many of the sailors ended their lives with the same disease, and of twenty-five officers who fell ill of yellow fever, twenty-three died. In the next eighty years, when our naval ships were ordered to the Caribbean, many another officer and seaman died of this same pestilence. In all the two hundred and fifty years yellow fever had been known and studied by the doctors, medical science knew nothing of how to treat it, to say nothing of how to prevent it.

The last notable American to die of yellow fever was the most famous of our cartoonists, Thomas Nast. After his artistic career was over, he accepted the post of Consul General in Ecuador. Before sailing, he drew a cartoon of himself arriving at his place of duty, bag in hand, but over his head he depicted a hooded specter, with outstretched claws, labeled "Yellow Jack." (That had long been the nickname for the disease.) Within a few months that clever cartoon came tragically true, and Thomas Nast lay dead of yellow fever.

That happened in 1902. But already, the year before, the conquering discovery had been made, and that is the story of Dr. Walter Reed. In the preceding sketch of Edward Jenner, it was noted that he obtained his medical education, not by going to a school of medicine, but by being apprenticed to a doctor, as was the custom in the eighteenth century. Walter Reed's own education as a boy was interrupted by the Civil War, but when that was over he went to Charlottesville and entered the University of Virginia at the age of sixteen. There he took only one year of academic work, followed by a single year of medical study. Therefore he was granted the degree of M.D. at the age of seventeen! Compared with the time and study it takes now for a young man to obtain his medical degree, this sounds almost as old-fashioned as Jenner's apprenticeship.

From the University of Virginia, young Walter went north to study in New York, and received a second M.D. from the Bellevue Hospital there. Then he took a job with the Health Department of Brooklyn. In 1874 he received a doctor's commission in the Army, becoming an Assistant Surgeon with the rank of First Lieutenant. Soon he was assigned to frontier duty in Arizona, where he stayed eleven years. Feeling the need of more study, he managed to get duty in Baltimore, examining recruits, with permission to study at the Johns Hopkins Medical School. There he became fascinated by the new science of bacteriology, and in 1893 he became a professor of this subject in a newly organized medical school in Washington.

Always in the front rank of medical progress, Reed was one of the earliest to champion the use of antitoxin for diphtheria, and he was selected chairman of a committee to study the causes of typhoid, which in those days was such a menace to army camps. Reed showed that flies and dust and contact are more important ways of spreading the disease than water. So when the Spanish American War came in 1898, this brilliant young army surgeon had already made a name for himself.

Also, the year before, he had begun a study of yellow fever. But it was in 1900, after the war, that this disease played havoc with the American army of occupation in Cuba. It had killed many thousands more American soldiers than Spanish bullets during the war. Soon Reed was appointed head of a commission of four army doctors to make a study of the cause and the means of transmission of yellow fever.

The theory of mosquitoes carrying the germs had been suggested as early as 1854, and it was repeated by a Dr. Carlos Finlay of Havana, but it had never been put to the test. It was necessary to experiment with human beings, just as it had been for Jenner and his vaccine theory. Two doctors of Reed's commission, Lazear and Carroll, volunteered to be guinea pigs for the test. They applied to themselves mosquitoes which had fed on yellow fever patients. Dr. Carroll had a bad case of yellow fever and, though he recovered, he was left with a damaged heart. Dr. Lazear developed the disease and died, a noble self-sacrifice to the cause of humanity.

Other heroes offered to risk their lives in the same cause, soldiers and civilian clerks. General Wood offered a monetary reward to those who would volunteer, but the attitude of them all was expressed by two men, Private Kissinger and a clerk named Moran: "We volunteer solely for the cause of humanity and in the interest of science. The one condition on which we volunteer is that we get no compensation for it."

"Gentlemen," responded Dr. Reed, raising his hand to his visor, "I salute you!" After the death of Dr. Lazear, Walter Reed said, "It's my turn to take a bite," but he was persuaded that since he was nearly fifty years old he must not run the risk.

Other carefully controlled tests he conducted proved that soldiers who slept in close contact with the clothing and bedding taken from yellow fever patients at the hospital contracted no illness. And that was an important discovery, contrary to general belief.

Reed's commission worked from June 25, 1900, to February 4, 1901. In that time he proved conclusively that yellow fever is transmitted by the bite of a certain type of mosquito. He proved, too, just how long it took for the virus to develop in the mosquito. The effects of his work were astonishingly quick. In 1900 there were 1400 cases of yellow fever in Havana alone; in the very next year there were only thirty-seven cases reported in all Cuba! If all swamps and stagnant pools were drained or sprayed, that meant that no more yellow-fever mosquitoes could breed. Soon the disease became unknown in the United States. In New Orleans, for example, it had been a perpetual curse; today it has long since been free of it. Control of yellow fever made possible the digging of the Panama Canal. In short, a great plague in the western world had been conquered wherever medical science was free to operate.

As for Dr. Reed, after he had finished his report on yellow fever he returned to Washington and went back to his Army Medical School. Later, he was appointed Professor of Pathology in Columbia University. Unhappily, while there he was attacked by the common illness, appendicitis, but he neglected the symptoms till too late. After five days he died, at the early age of fifty-one.

His passing was mourned, not only because of what he had achieved but because he was greatly beloved as a man. He was quick to give full credit to the men who helped him, and was always modest about himself. Many honors came to him in his lifetime, and in his death he was buried with the war heroes in Arlington National Cemetery. And the great general hospital in Washington is named "Walter Reed" in his honor.

SAMUEL GRIDLEY HOWE
HELEN ADAMS KELLER

SAMUEL G. HOWE

HELEN KELLER

III. SAMUEL GRIDLEY HOWE

November 10, 1801—January 9, 1876

HELEN ADAMS KELLER

January 27, 1880—

No one who knew Sam Howe as a boy in Boston would ever have dreamed that one day he would be a famous humanitarian. He was a mischievous young daredevil from the time he could walk. In boyhood, his favorite playground was the yard or "rope-walk" at his father's place of business on the bank of the Charles River. Sam's favorite sport after the big spring thaw was to jump from one ice cake to another on the river without falling in. He was clever and a good jumper, but once he did fall in, and his father had to plunge into the icy water and fish the boy out. "Go home, Sam," said the parent sternly, "and tell your mother to give you a whipping." Sam ran home dripping and he told his mother; but, as he wrote in later life, "she did not give me the whipping."

If his mother spared him, his principal at the Boston Latin School certainly did not. This man must have been a brute. Once, because he saw that Sam took his beatings without tears, he whacked the boy's hand into a bloody pulp, just to make him cry. But Sam managed to keep his tears back, nevertheless.

One trouble at this school was that practically everybody, from the principal down, was a Federalist, the party of John Adams. But Sam's father was one of the few Democrats—the party of Jefferson—living in Boston at that time. Sam was therefore constantly involved in fights on the playground with the other boys who tried to beat him up because of his father's politics. Once a gang of his schoolmates threw him head first down the stairs, and that time the principal was looking on with full approval!

Sam's father had a prosperous business making cordage for ships in those days of sailing vessels, and during the War of 1812 he had his hands full with orders for the American Navy. But after the war our government conveniently forgot to pay him. That piece of dishonesty on the part of Congress meant near ruin for the business, so that when the three Howe boys were ready for college, the father announced that he could afford to send only one. He called them together one day. "Here," said he, opening the big family Bible, "I want each of you to read aloud. The one who reads best will be the boy to go to college."

There was no doubt about it, Sam read his passage with better expression than his brothers. "Sam, you'll go," was the verdict. All the other Boston boys went to Harvard as a matter of course, but Mr. Howe declared that it was just a nest of Federalists. Instead, Sam was sent off in a bumpy stagecoach to Providence, Rhode Island, to enroll at Brown University, a Baptist college, which the elder Howe thought would be a friendlier place for Democrats.

At college Sam was quick at his studies, but he made a name for himself as a prankster, always up to some practical joke. Years after he had graduated, he went to call on his old college president, then living in retirement. The old gentleman eyed Sam with evident alarm and moved his chair back. "I declare, Howe," said he, "I am afraid of you even now. I'm afraid there will be a torpedo under my chair before I know it." (The word torpedo in those days meant a floating mine used to blow up ships.)

Sam graduated from Brown in 1821. Soon there came news of the Greek war of independence against the Turks, and the whole free world was excited and sympathetic. In 1823, the English poet, Lord Byron, went to Greece to volunteer his services. After graduating from Brown, Sam had gone to the Harvard Medical School and received his M.D. degree in 1824. The news from Greece stirred his adventurous spirit. He had read about Lord Byron.

Samuel Gridley Howe

Certainly the Greek rebels needed a doctor-surgeon much more than a poet in the war. So off he went, in the winter of 1824-25, as a young crusader for liberty. This, in spite of his father's stern disapproval.

Six exciting years were spent in the cause of Greece. One year of that time he devoted to a mission to America to plead for help. There was a warm response, and he rushed back with a whole shipload of food, clothing and medicines which the Greek forces needed desperately. Just before the young American doctor arrived back in Greece, Lord Byron died of a fever. In the sale of the poet's effects, Sam bought Byron's helmet, a steel headpiece inlaid with gold and decorated with a romantic blue plume. A hundred years later, Samuel Howe's descendants presented it to the museum in Athens, and there it is now, resting on a cushion in a glass case.

While in Greece, during the year 1830, Samuel Howe also was laid low with a fever and nearly died. He felt the effects of that terrible illness all the rest of his life. On his way home, he happened to be in Paris at the time of a little three-day revolution which pushed one stupid king off the throne of France and substituted another one equally stupid. A born rebel, Howe joined the crowd marching on the City Hall, but Lafayette, who was at the head of the procession, noticed him and said, "Young man, reserve yourself for the needs of your own country. This is *our* battle!"

The spring of 1831 found the young physician back in Boston, a doctor with a record of romantic adventures in Greece but with no practice. However, he had made such a reputation for himself that various people came to him offering different kinds of opportunities. It was clear that this young knight, "without fear and without reproach," was not the sort of person to be satisfied with a humdrum medical practice. Whatever Samuel Howe undertook would have to be a Cause, a Crusade.

It happened that in 1829 the Massachusetts legislature had passed a law establishing a New England Asylum for the Blind. By the time Howe was back in Boston, a few trustees had been appointed. One of these, in fact, went to Paris to study at the Institute for the Blind there, a school for blind youth that later became famous as the institution where Louis Braille, inventor of the famous Braille alphabet, studied and taught. On the return of this trustee, he and his two colleagues one day were talking over the problem of electing a man to be the head of this asylum for the blind in Boston, when they happened to see Dr. Howe passing. "There's our man!" one of the men cried out. And the others agreed.

At that time Samuel Howe was thirty years old, in the prime of his manhood, tall, erect, soldierly, with jet black hair, fine features and flashing blue eyes. Many years later an old lady wrote of him as "the handsomest man in Boston. When he rode by on his black horse, all the girls ran to the windows to look after him." Added to those fine looks was great force of character, a strong will, and remarkable personal magnetism.

The matter was brought to his attention. A school for the blind? Why, here was a Cause to work for, not just a living. He accepted the post. In those days nothing was being done for blind children anywhere in America. Howe realized that he knew nothing about teaching the blind and that there was no one in Boston to instruct him, but he saw a great opportunity. He would learn all there was to learn, and maybe go ahead to still better methods.

First he made a trip to Europe to study the work being done there, especially at the Institute for the Blind in Paris. But he went elsewhere as well. And in one of his journeys he got into trouble with the Prussian police because he had brought aid to some Polish refugees. The young American crusader found himself in jail, and there he was kept for six weeks! And all the while he was required to pay the jailer for his board! Years afterward, when he was famous the world over, the King of Prussia awarded him a gold medal. Out of curiosity, Howe had the medal valued and he discovered, to his great amusement, that it came to exactly the sum of money he had paid his Prussian jailer for food.

In 1832 he opened the school for the blind, in the house he had inherited from his father, with six blind pupils. It had to be pioneer work. At first Howe went about with his eyes bandaged, just to be able to understand what it meant to be blind. He spent long hours with bits of twine and glue, twisting them into shapes of letters stuck to sheets of cardboard so that the blind children could learn the alphabet with their fingertips. At that time printing with raised or

Samuel Gridley Howe

embossed type had been invented, but there were only three books so printed in English; one a collection of pieces from English authors, one a treatise on Christian doctrines, and the third, the Gospel of St. John. Today the institution that Samuel Howe founded has in its library 20,000 books for the blind, although the embossed type has long since been superseded by Braille. But from the very first, Dr. Howe gave his pupils something far more important than string-made alphabets. Every child came to think of him as a loving father, and all caught from him his spirit of courage and hope. He would never let the children feel sorry for themselves. The guiding motto of the institution from the very first was "Obstacles are things to overcome."

In a short time Samuel Howe discovered that he himself had obstacles to overcome. All the money he had for his school was gone in six months, and there was a debt of three hundred dollars. Out he went to publicize the work for the blind, and such was the charm of his personality and the persuasiveness of his argument that money came pouring in. Ladies of near-by cities as well as Boston held fairs to raise money for his work. A prominent citizen named Perkins offered his big house for the school if Howe could raise $50,000. That was a huge sum of money a hundred years ago, but Samuel Howe was equal to anything. He raised the money and moved the school to the Perkins mansion, which thereafter became known as the Perkins Institute, in honor of the donor.

By 1839 the Institute had outgrown even the big Perkins house. Thereupon Dr. Howe bought a large hotel then on the market. In that building the Perkins Institute remained for seventy-three years. In all this work he had as his helper his sister Jennette, who acted as his housekeeper and companion. In 1843 he married a beautiful girl, Julia Ward. At that time she was twenty-two and he was forty. In spite of the difference in their ages, it proved to be a very happy marriage. And Mrs. Howe herself became famous some twenty years later by her stirring marching song, composed during our Civil War, "The Battle Hymn of the Republic." Thereafter, when she visited the school the children would sing the chorus of that hymn, but would change it to "Glory, glory, Julia Ward Howe" in her honor.

Famous Humanitarians

Meanwhile, in 1837, Dr. Howe heard of a girl living on a farm near Hanover, New Hampshire, who was not only blind but deaf and dumb. The poor child had suffered a severe attack of scarlet fever which had taken away sight, speech and hearing. Her name was Laura Bridgman. Dr. Howe readily obtained her parents' consent to take her into the Perkins Institute, and in time she became his most famous pupil. Howe worked with her with as much devotion as if she had been his own child, teaching her slowly, step by step. Through his efforts she grew up intelligent, happy, and active. She made a name for herself as the most expert needlewoman in Boston. Naturally, all her life she felt the deepest love and reverence for her teacher. Her story alone made Samuel Howe famous all over the civilized world.

After a time there came another call on his skill and kindliness. He found blind children who were also feeble-minded. At first he took them into the Perkins Institute, but he soon found out that it was not wise to mix normal blind children with the sub-normal blind. So he bought a lot in South Boston and put up a building for the latter. At that time nobody did anything for such children, but Howe learned to make even these poor creatures happy. Of course he was faithful to his duties at Perkins, but he never missed a day at this second institution, which presented a far more difficult problem.

Dr. Howe's life was so full that it is difficult to compress its story into a few pages. He was the friend of all the distinguished citizens of New England in those days—writers, statesmen, clergymen, leaders of great causes. On the morning of January 4, 1876, he left home, as usual, to walk to the Institute. He had gone only a few steps when he fell, suddenly stricken. After a few days in bed he passed on. Tributes of honor came from all sides. John Greenleaf Whittier wrote a poem about him entitled "The Hero," and at a great public meeting in honor of Samuel Howe held on the February 8th following, Oliver Wendell Holmes read a poem of his own, "A Memorial Tribute." Two stanzas of this were:

> "He touched the eyelids of the blind,
>   And lo! the veil withdrawn,
> As o'er the midnight of the mind
>   He led the light of dawn.

Helen Adams Keller

"No labored line, no sculptor's art
Such hallowed memory needs;
His tablet is the human heart,
His record loving deeds."

Helen Adams Keller

Samuel Gridley Howe was born over one hundred and fifty years ago, but to show how his work continues we have the living example of one who has become far better known than even Laura Bridgman in her day, a person who may be called the spiritual grandchild of Samuel Gridley Howe. Mark Twain once said, "The two most interesting characters of the nineteenth century are Napoleon and Helen Keller." When he said that, she was only fifteen years old, but already a great work had been done in releasing a terribly afflicted child to something like a normal life.

Helen Keller was born a normal baby in the town of Tuscumbia, Alabama. When she was nineteen months old she had scarlet fever, which left her, as the same disease had done for Laura Bridgman, blind, deaf and dumb.

The parents felt helpless as they watched their little girl grow up like an animal. But Dr. Alexander Graham Bell, the inventor of the telephone, heard of the pitiful case and suggested that Mr. Keller write to the Perkins Institute in Boston. He told of all that Dr. Howe had done for Laura Bridgman many years before. This brought a ray of hope, and Helen's father wrote to the head of Perkins, asking him to send someone qualified to teach the child as Dr. Howe had taught Laura. It happened that there was a young woman at the Institute who had been sent there when she had a serious eye disease. She had stayed six years and by this time was able to see normally. Her name was Anne Sullivan. "Annie," said the Superintendent of the Institute, "this looks like a job for you." At the time she was only twenty and had never taken charge of a blind child, to say nothing of one that was blind, deaf and dumb. "I'll try," she replied bravely, and off she went on the long journey to Alabama.

She found Helen a tousled, dirty, bad-tempered little child, who at first fought against her. That was in March, 1887. Such was the magic of Anne

Famous Humanitarians

Sullivan's teaching that by July of that very year Helen Keller was able to talk fluently with her fingers, could read raised type, and write a clear script. There followed a rich life. Helen and her teacher became inseparable. Thanks to Miss Sullivan's help, Helen was able to go to preparatory school and then enter Radcliffe. And when she graduated it was *cum laude*. Her final examinations were put before her in the type invented by Braille which is now in universal use for the blind. She felt out the questions with fingertips and wrote her answers in the clear, square script Anne Sullivan had taught her.

Thereafter Helen Keller's life was not spent in the Institute, as Laura Bridgman's had been, but out in the world, just as if she were a normal person. She has counted among her friends such men as Edward Everett Hale, Bishop Phillips Brooks and Mark Twain. She has championed Woman's Suffrage and has continued to support every good cause she could serve. At the Horace Mann school in New York she was taught to speak, and so overcame another great disability. She has even braved with success the lecture platform. Her sense of touch is so finely developed that it has almost conquered her deafness, for she has learned to enjoy music by the vibrations on her fingertips as she rests them on a piano or violin or on the throat of a singer. These and other amazing achievements Miss Keller has won with the help of Miss Sullivan and other teachers, plus her own determination. She has lived up grandly to Dr. Howe's motto for Perkins Institute, "Obstacles are made to be overcome."

Like the Frenchman, Louis Braille, who, being blind, devoted his life to helping the blind, Miss Keller has put her all into the same great cause. She has served on many commissions for the blind. She raised a million dollars to endow a Foundation for the Blind, and to that great service she still devotes her time and talents. She has the spirit of Dr. Howe, though handicapped by such physical afflictions as no other humanitarian ever had to overcome.

Through Anne Sullivan, this rich life traces back to Perkins Institute and the knightly man who founded it. Helen Keller has inherited not only his teaching methods but also the spirit of devotion to the afflicted that was his lifelong passion. And that is why it can be said of her that she is spiritually the granddaughter of Samuel Gridley Howe.

DOROTHEA LYNDE DIX

DOROTHEA DIX

IV. DOROTHEA LYNDE DIX

April 4, 1802—July 17, 1887

THIS "GENTLE WARRIOR," as she was called in her lifetime, must not be confused with a famous newspaper woman of a later day, Elizabeth Meriwether, who covered sensational murder trials and conducted a column of personal advice, especially to the lovelorn. She took Dorothy Dix for her pen name, long after the real Dorothea Dix had died. As a matter of fact, the latter was christened Dorothy, but changed it later to Dorothea which she liked better.

The Dorothea Lynde Dix who is the subject of this chapter made herself internationally famous as the person who did more than anyone else to better the treatment of the insane, especially in America. One who wrote her story called her a "Forgotten Samaritan," because it is true that, although she was indeed a good Samaritan to the neglected and abused insane, she seems now to be largely forgotten.

Before beginning her life story, it is necessary to say something about the historical background of the weak-minded folk and the way they were treated. The father of medical science, the Greek Hippocrates, as long ago as five hundred years before Christ, declared that insanity was a disease of the brain. The same thought was repeated by that other great pioneer of medicine, another Greek named Galen, who lived six centuries later. But in Europe that sensible idea was set aside for another theory which was supposed to come out of the Bible. During many centuries of the Christian era, insanity was thought to be caused by the presence in a person of an evil spirit. And the way to get rid of that devil was to make the afflicted one so miserable by beatings, vile insults, filthy doses and smells—every imaginable ill treatment —that the evil spirit would be so disgusted with the body he had entered that he would get out. The fact that this theory never worked was overlooked.

Outside Europe, the treatment of the insane was no better. Until modern times in India, for example, the insane were let down into snake-pits crawling with deadly cobras. If by some very rare chance the snakes were too sluggish to bite, the poor lunatic would be hauled up and sent to some shrine as a holy man.

Gradually, during the Middle Ages, a more merciful attitude came about, in spite of the evil spirit theory. The Christian Church set up a number of hospitals for the care of the insane under the direction of religious orders. The most famous of these for English-speaking peoples was the Hospital of Saint Mary of Bethlehem, founded in London in 1246. When, in the sixteenth century, Henry VIII broke up the religious houses, this institution fell into the control of the city officials of London. The name gradually became shortened to "Bedlam," a word that now means loud, confused voices. This meaning came about because of the shrieks and screams of the unhappy inmates.

No one seemed sorry for these inmates after the Church lost control. Even as late as the eighteenth century, these insane persons were exhibited like wild animals in a zoo. There were long rows of them chained to the walls of the corridors. Admission was charged, and it was a popular Sunday afternoon pastime for Londoners to go to Bedlam to have a good laugh at the demented creatures with their crazy speech and actions. If any one didn't perform, just stayed quiet, it was all right to give him a jab with a cane or umbrella until he howled. It was all considered very comical! In contrast with that picture, the present London hospital for the insane is a completely modern asylum, with a record of sending away more than half of the patients cured of their mental ills. The credit for the difference between this hospital and the Bedlam of one hundred and fifty years ago can be shared by two humanitarians, the Earl of Shaftesbury in England and Dorothea Dix in America.

Dorothea Dix was born on April 4, 1802, in a small farm settlement in Maine called Hamden, about six miles below Bangor. The village was on the

Dorothea Lynde Dix

edge of a timber tract owned by Dorothea's grandfather, a successful doctor, shipowner, man of business and public-spirited citizen of Boston. He had sent his son to be a sort of agent for him, to look out for his lumber interests. But that son was a good-for-nothing. For a time he was a drunkard and then became a religious fanatic. He never could hold a job; all the money he could make was a few cents from the sale of his sermons. Much of Dorothea's girlhood was spent in stitching together the pages of these sermons to save the cost of binding. She hated the work, and in consequence took harsh words from her mother and beatings with a rattan from her father. "I never knew childhood," she wrote in later years, and it was bitterly true. She never would talk about her unhappy life in her own home.

Indeed, she was so miserable that she eventually packed up and left for her grandparents' home in Boston. Dr. Dix had died when she was only seven, but the grandmother lived on in the handsome brick house known as the Dix Mansion. There the unhappy girl found not only physical comfort but a love and kindness which she had never had from her own parents.

After a while, the grandmother sent Dorothea to her great-aunt's home in Worcester, Massachusetts. When she was fourteen she announced that she was going to teach school. In spite of family objections and her youth, she went ahead and carried on for a year a school for young children. But she had larger ambitions. After that year she went back to Grandmother Dix in Boston, and persuaded the old lady to let her set up a day and boarding school for girls in the big house. In those days there was quite a demand for girls' schools because the public schools had room for girls only during the summer months when many of the boys went to work. In her school Dorothea employed only one assistant, a teacher of French and Latin. All the other subjects she herself handled. And, having had little education herself, she buried herself in books to fit herself for her work.

One day, as she was coming home from a library with an armful of books, she came to a windy corner, and a gust whipped at her cape and skirt so hard that she dropped a volume. As she stooped to pick it up, a man's arm reached it first and a kind voice said, "Aeolus [in mythology the ruler of the winds] always gets the upper hand here, doesn't he?" Looking into the stranger's face, she instantly recognized the best known and most beloved man in Boston, Dr. William Ellery Channing, a Unitarian minister with a national reputation. He talked to Dorothea about her reading, she told him about her school, and there on that windy street corner began a friendship that proved invaluable to the young schoolmistress. Dr. Channing sent his daughters to Dorothea's school, and she, in turn, became a member of his congregation as well as a frequent visitor in his home. Much of the inspiration to make her life one of unselfish helpfulness to those in need came from him.

Besides keeping school, Dorothea somehow found time to write books for children, long forgotten now but popular then. All this meant overwork and a breakdown with a racking cough. In the spring of 1836 she had to close the school. The Channings invited her to their summer home on Narragansett Bay, where she could tutor the children, and for the next six months she was a member of the Channing household. Then, still in search of health, she went to Europe, but the voyage was so rough that she landed in Liverpool too weak to stand. There some friends of the Channings took her into their beautiful country home, and insisted on her staying with them for the next eighteen months.

All this while, and she was now in her middle thirties, she had not dreamed of the work that was destined to make her famous. She was just another New England schoolmarm. While she was in England, her grandmother died. But when she returned to Boston after her long rest abroad, she was not alone, because through Dr. Channing she counted among her friends the most famous men and women in Massachusetts at that time, such as John Greenleaf Whittier; Julia Ward Howe, the poet, and her husband, Dr. Samuel Ward Howe, the teacher of the blind; Senator Charles Sumner, and many another eminent figure in various walks of life.

It was in March, 1841, when Dorothea was nearing her fortieth birthday, that she volunteered to take a Sunday School class that no one else wanted because it was in the House of Correction, the women's jail in East Cambridge (Massachusetts). In taking over this class of twenty women, which of course was held in the jail, she discovered that along with the inmates who had been sentenced for bad conduct there were insane persons as well. These afflicted

Dorothea Lynde Dix

ones were housed in an unheated room, no matter what the temperature was outside. She protested to the jail officers, but with no success. Then she took the matter to court and there succeeded in getting some action on behalf of these lunatics. Thereafter, for the next ten years, she went about the state of Massachusetts investigating the treatment of the insane. In 1843 she presented a report to the legislature, telling the lawmakers about "the present state of the insane, persons confined within this commonwealth in cages, closets, cellars, stalls, pens, chained, naked, beaten with rods and lashed into obedience." She described how these inmates were crowded together in filth, with no ventilation, living like animals on wet straw, in pens that in winter were white with frost crystals.

This report startled not only the legislature, but also the public, because Dorothea Dix gave the facts to the newspapers also. Finally, she got a bill passed to enlarge the Worcester asylum and make it a decent place. That was only the beginning, as she came to realize that the treatment of the insane in Massachusetts was not a bit worse than that in any other state. In 1843 she began a tour of inspection over the entire country. And that, in those days, was no pleasure jaunt. Most of it was by river steamboat or stagecoach, chiefly the latter. Roads in those days were so bad that a long coach journey was a matter of real danger as well as fatigue. Time and again her stagecoach broke down. After a number of these accidents, she always carried with her a repair outfit—hammer, wrench, nails, screws, a coil of rope and stout leather straps. These saved the day in many a road accident that followed. Fording rivers was another peril, and there was always the danger of being held up by highwaymen.

A biographer of Dorothea Dix tells the following story of how she handled one such incident. One day when getting into a coach she noticed that the driver had pistols. "Why?" she demanded.

"Robbers on the road," was the reply.

"Give me the pistols," she ordered. And such was her personality that the man meekly obeyed. On that journey a highwayman did step out on the road and, stopping the horses, he demanded money at the point of a pistol. The lady passenger took over.

Famous Humanitarians

"Aren't you ashamed of this business?" she asked gently. "But if you have been unfortunate and are in real need, I'll give you some money."

"Oh, that voice!" the robber exclaimed. He suddenly realized that he had heard her speak to the convicts when he was confined in a Pennsylvania prison. He shook his head and begged her to go on, refusing her offer of money.

"Take it," she insisted, "because without it you might be tempted to rob again before you get employment."

There was no refusing Dorothea Dix. He took the money gratefully and slipped away among the trees.

That tour of inspection covered over ten thousand miles in three and a half years, and only ten years before the doctors had given her up as a hopeless invalid, doomed to early death. In this tour she visited eighteen state prisons, over five hundred poorhouses, three hundred county jails, besides many so-called hospitals and houses of refuge. With the facts that she assembled, she won over, in the following years, the legislatures of Indiana, Illinois, Kentucky, Tennessee, Missouri, Massachusetts, Louisiana, Alabama, South Carolina, North Carolina and Maryland, to set up special hospitals for the insane. And all this she achieved singlehanded!

Of course, she had a wonderfully winning personality. She was fine-looking, tall, blue-eyed, with handsome features. In her youth she had had an unhappy love affair, after which she gave up the idea of marriage. In her day there were other women reformers fighting the causes of temperance, women's suffrage, and abolition of slavery, but some of these were loud and angry on the platform or addressing legislatures. Dorothea's voice was always low and gentle. She avoided public lectures in favor of talking to groups or individuals in a friendly, winning way. Sometimes she would appeal to rich philanthropists as well as legislators, and she got results this way, too.

Certainly her crusade was sorely needed. In her report of what she had seen in her country-wide tour, she told of "more than 9,000 idiots, epileptics and insane . . . destitute of care and protection, in jails and poorhouses . . . thousands bound with chains, fetters, and iron balls attached to heavy chains, lacerated with ropes, beaten with rods," and lying in filth. With this noble woman began the humane and scientific treatment of the insane in America, treatment looking for cure, and something that even one hundred years ago was thought impossible for sick minds.

From the American scene Miss Dix went to inspect treatment of the insane in Europe. There she found much the same conditions as at home. In Edinburgh she came upon dreadful abuses in private asylums. When she made her report to the Lord Provost of the city, she got no response, but Queen Victoria became interested and appointed a royal commission which brought about much needed reforms.

All the time that she was at work on this mission for the insane, she never missed an opportunity to do something for other good causes. For instance, in 1853, while she was working to establish a hospital in St. Johns, Newfoundland, she heard of the dangerous shoals of Sable Island, lying far off the Nova Scotia coast, that had caused many wrecks and great loss of life. There was no lighthouse, and little lifesaving apparatus was available. She went to the island to see for herself, a rough and risky journey for a woman. Then she went to the merchants of Philadelphia, Boston and New York, asking for money to set up a proper lifesaving station there. As usual she succeeded, and within a week of the arrival of that equipment on the island a ship with one hundred and sixty-eight persons was saved.

Her one cruel disappointment came when, after Congress had passed a bill setting aside lands for the care of the insane through taxes, President Pierce vetoed it. If she had been able to talk to him, we may be sure it would have been a different story.

When the Civil War broke out, she volunteered her services and was appointed Superintendent of Women Nurses. She served all through the war, selecting the personnel of the nurses and assigning them to various military hospitals. As might be expected, she managed this duty splendidly, even though she always referred to it in later years as only an episode in her life.

The war over, back she went to inspecting and traveling in order to create hospitals for the insane. In her eightieth year she retired to a home, offered her by what she called her "first child," a hospital she had created in Trenton, New Jersey. Here, on July 17, 1887, this "Gentle Warrior" ended her life story. She had fought a long campaign for the most unhappy and neglected members of the human race, those that are sick in mind. Toward the end she still longed to be of service to others, and said once, "I think, even lying in my bed, I can still do something." Her work lives on today, for all the kindly and modern scientific care of the insane in America dates from the life of this devoted woman. It is singularly appropriate that she should have borne the name Dorothea, because it means "Gift of God."

WILLIAM LLOYD GARRISON
HARRIET BEECHER STOWE

WILLIAM LLOYD GARRISON

HARRIET BEECHER STOWE

V. WILLIAM LLOYD GARRISON

December 10, 1805—May 24, 1879

HARRIET BEECHER STOWE

June 14, 1811—July 1, 1896

THE TWO NAMES at the head of this chapter are the most prominent in the story of the anti-slavery movement in the United States. The practice of slavery is older than the dawn of history. It probably began by making a prisoner of war a sort of work animal instead of putting him to death. Then it developed into a big business, in which savage lands were raided for men and women to sell in the labor market. It was the labor of slaves that built the great monuments of antiquity, such as the pyramids of Egypt and the roads and aqueducts of imperial Rome.

After the discovery of the New World, there was a great demand for slaves to do the heavy manual work on the plantations. Since the native Indian refused to submit to slavery, the labor had to be brought in from elsewhere. The chief source had always been Africa, which had supplied Egypt with Negro slaves at least as early as 3000 B.C. And the Dark Continent remained for centuries an inexhaustible supply.

After the colonization of America and the West Indies, the demand for slaves was so great that the slave trade became highly profitable. In fact, the city of Liverpool in England owed its growth and early prosperity to the slave ships that it owned, plying between the west coast of Africa and the ports of the New World. In this traffic the slavers had as their partners the Negro chiefs of the tribes living near the coast. They would raid neighboring tribes and carry off men and women to sell to the slave traders. Sometimes these chiefs would even sell their own people. Dr. Moton, late principal of Tuskegee Institute, was the grandson of a Zulu chief who was deep in this business but who made the mistake one day of stepping aboard a slave ship with his gang of victims. The captain promptly clapped him in irons, too, and brought him to America.

The first cargo of Negroes shipped to the American colonies arrived at Jamestown in 1619. Then and thereafter, for nearly two hundred years, slavery was taken as a matter of course, North as well as South. The practice died out in the Northern colonies since it was not profitable on small farms. But it flourished in the South because of the need for large gangs of laborers on the large plantations raising rice, tobacco, and cotton.

Beginning with the English Quakers, however, there dawned the idea that the institution was wrong; that no human being, unless convicted of crime, should be owned like an ox or a mule, to be worked without wages all his life at the whim of the owner. When news of the French Revolution came to the West Indies, the Negroes of Haiti and Martinique rose in rebellion and killed their masters with their families in a frightful massacre. This tragic event helped to draw the attention of the world to the whole question of slavery. The protest of the Quakers in England was quickly echoed among the Quakers in America, and the sentiment against slavery began to spread.

The first step taken was to forbid slavery in the Northwest Territory in 1787, and then to end by law the horrible slave trade. In 1807, Congress forbade the traffic by law, to take effect January 1, 1808. But the business was so profitable that "bootlegging" in slaves went on right up to our Civil War. Britain stood with us in outlawing the slave trade, and then in 1833, Parliament, under the leadership of Bishop Wilberforce, abolished slavery in British colonies. This was done by appropriating twenty million pounds to compensate the owners for their slaves, and these planters were allowed to keep their slaves on for another seven years on an apprenticeship basis, to ease the passing from slave to free labor.

William Lloyd Garrison

In our country, the Southern states passed laws to protect the rights of slaves and guarantee them good treatment. Yet in the early years of the nineteenth century, there were many in the South who did not like the practice of slavery, and it is only fair to note that, in 1825, out of 143 emancipation societies in the United States, 103 were in Southern states. But later, with the invention of the cotton gin and improvements in crop cultivation, it seemed to Southerners like John C. Calhoun that the prosperity of their section of the country was dependent on slave labor. Finally, the problem tore the two sections of the nation apart and had to be settled by a terrible war.

The man who made himself famous as the most violent enemy of slavery, William Lloyd Garrison, was born in Newburyport, Massachusetts. His father was a drunken sea captain who deserted his family before the boy was three. After only a little schooling, the lad was apprenticed at thirteen to a printer, and for the unusually long period of seven years. But that gave him time to become an expert typesetter.

Naturally, this kind of work led him to the idea of printing a paper of his own. And so he started a little sheet which is remembered now chiefly because on its pages William printed the early poems of John Greenleaf Whittier. This early contact led to a lifelong friendship between these two men.

After the speedy death of this paper, young Garrison went to Boston to find a job as printer, and before long he was editing another paper with the ambitious title, *The National Philanthropist*. With this he began his career as a reformer, attacking "intemperance and kindred vices." One of these was tobacco, another was the theater, and still another was Sabbath breaking.

At that time there was in Baltimore a Quaker named Lundy who was editing a paper which argued for a gradual end to slavery. But he decided that his editorials didn't have the necessary punch; nobody paid any attention to them. Having by an odd chance seen a copy of Garrison's publication, which had plenty of punch in it, he walked all the way from Baltimore to Bennington, Vermont, where the young man had moved and was then getting out his paper. Lundy persuaded him to come to Baltimore and start a vigorous crusade against slavery in Lundy's paper.

That was the year 1829, and once Garrison got to writing the editorials, there was no more talk about gradual emancipation. His language was so violent against slave-holders that it brought him to court. There he was convicted of libel and fined fifty dollars and costs. Not having fifty dollars, he went to jail. But after a while someone came along who paid the fine, and Garrison was set free. The jail sentence made him a martyr, at least in his own eyes, but he didn't want that to happen again. So back North he went to begin a series of lectures against slavery. He wasn't welcome there, either. His own native town of Newburyport closed its doors against his talk; even the churches refused to let him speak from their platforms. He was, they all said, a firebrand and a troublemaker.

Nevertheless, he went ahead and founded an anti-slavery society. He became its salaried agent, and in 1833 that society sent him to England. That was the very year in which the British emancipated the slaves in their colonies by paying the owners, as described earlier. The young American reformer condemned any compensation to slave-holders, and in his lecture tour he cursed the wickedness of his native land, especially on this issue of slavery. This kind of talk made him more popular in England than in America.

Two years later, an Englishman named Thompson came to America to tell us how bad we were on this question of slavery. He was scheduled to speak in Philadelphia, where Garrison had founded an anti-slavery society, after being driven out of New York by an angry mob. The Englishman was tipped off that there would be trouble, and he stayed away, but Garrison was there. A mob seized him, pulled him out of the hall, tore the clothes off his back and dragged him through the streets with a rope around his neck. He would have been tarred and feathered, at least, and might even have been killed, as Elijah Lovejoy was by a mob in Alton, Illinois, two years later, but the Mayor stepped in and sent Garrison to jail for safe-keeping.

In 1840 he went to England again; but when he was told there that no women were allowed to speak in the hall, he himself refused to speak, for Women's Rights was one of his secondary issues. In that year he was elected president of the Anti-Slavery Society and he held that office for twenty-two years, until slavery was no more.

There is no doubt that Garrison was a real fanatic, so much so that many people who opposed slavery turned against him. To him, every one who owned a slave was a devil with hoofs and horns. He argued for the North to secede from the South. He called the Constitution "a covenant with death and a compact with hell." Once he publicly burned a copy of that document, shouting, "So perish all compromise with tyranny!" He attacked the Bible because in it slavery was accepted, not denounced. He even called orthodox churches "cages of unclean birds, Augean stables of pollution." Because an Irish temperance orator, Father Matthew, and the Hungarian patriot, Louis Kossuth, then visiting in this country, would not denounce slavery, he cursed them both in abusive language. He wouldn't even support Lincoln until after the Emancipation Proclamation.

Naturally, all this bitter name-calling by the Abolitionists, for whom he set the example, bred resentment and hatred in the South, and all hope of a peaceful, gradual end to slavery, such as had happened in the British colonies, became impossible. The actual freeing of the slaves was not the work of William Lloyd Garrison. Slavery as an institution was wrong; even at best it could not be justified as a practice, and we must remember this man for his courage in fighting for emancipation during the years when the idea was unpopular in the North as well as in the South, and when it meant risk of bodily harm and perhaps death. Even when a mob was dragging him through the streets, it never occurred to him to yield an inch on his principles.

Harriet Beecher Stowe

The other name chiefly associated with the anti-slavery movement in America is Harriet Beecher Stowe. Daughter of a Congregational minister in Litchfield, Connecticut, and sister of a much more famous one, Henry Ward Beecher, she grew up in a stern, puritanical atmosphere. As a girl she was fascinated by an uncle, Sam Foote, who, to her, was a daring and romantic figure. He followed the sea, and he dared to say that on his travels he learned that Turks are as good as Christians and Catholics as good as Protestants. Such bold talk made Hattie Beecher thrill. And she was never afterward afraid of thinking differently from the people around her. Her interest in colored people came from the fact that in her childhood she had a step-mother whom she feared, and, as a result, she had turned for mother love to two kindly Negro women, one the washerwoman and the other the cook, in the Beecher home.

When she was twenty-one, her father moved to Cincinnati, where he became head of a theological seminary, and where her sister Catherine founded a school for girls. Harriet became a teacher in that school. It was not long before she tried her hand at writing, and she won fifty dollars for a story that she sent to the *Western Monthly Magazine*.

In 1836 she married a professor in her father's seminary, Calvin Stowe. And then for a long time she dropped writing, being too busy as a wife and mother. When her husband urged her to try again with her pen, she said that she had no inspiration, no ideas. Six of her seven children were born during the eighteen years that she lived in Cincinnati. One of these died in a cholera epidemic. It was during this period of her life that she made a visit to the South, chiefly in Kentucky, and there she had a glimpse of slave life in planta-tion cabins. Apparently, what she saw increased her opposition to slavery.

In 1850 her husband became a professor at Bowdoin College in Maine. On her way north and east, she saw her brother Henry, pastor at the Plymouth Church in Brooklyn, and he urged her to write something for the anti-slavery cause. She decided to try. From June, 1851, to April, 1852, a story of hers was printed in *The National Era*, an anti-slavery paper in Washington. The tale was called *Uncle Tom's Cabin, or Life Among the Lowly*. In those days Washington was distinctly a Southern city, and it was for a long time the center of a prosperous interstate trade in slaves. But so few people read the paper that it made no stir. In 1852, however, the story came out as a book. Instantly it made a sensation, selling half a million copies in the next five years here, and tens of thousands as well in England. From there it went into a score of European translations.

Southerners at once were ablaze with indignation at what they called a wicked misrepresentation of slavery in the South, and even moderate North-erners felt that Mrs. Stowe had gone too far. In reply, she published the following year a "Key" to *Uncle Tom's Cabin,* to show that she had based the incidents on what she had reason to believe had really happened. Uncle Tom himself was the portrait of a runaway slave whom she had met.

The author thought that she had been fair to the South because she had made the brutal Simon Legree a Yankee, and had pictured, in the Shelbys and St. Clairs, slave-owners who were kind. But the impression left on every reader was mainly that of bloodhounds, whips, and abuse of slaves, even to death. We know now that the vast majority of slave-holders were kind, God-fearing people, who cared for their "servants," as they preferred to call them, in sickness and old age, and won their devoted loyalty. Abolitionists never could understand why the slaves refused to rise under John Brown and murder their white folks as the slaves had done in Haiti, or why, when all the men were away in the Confederate armies, their slaves stayed, for the most part, where they were, loyal to their masters' families.

The widespread success of *Uncle Tom's Cabin* was due to its being an interesting story, with characters that seemed real, like the unforgettable Topsy. And it is strange that although Mrs. Stowe tried again and again, she never could write another story to compare with it. But this one book was sufficient to place Harriet Beecher Stowe among the few women in our national Hall of Fame.

We have seen already how Great Britain accomplished a peaceful emancipation of the slaves in her colonies by paying the owners a compensation for the loss of their human property. This method was fought bitterly by Garrison and most of the other Abolitionists who shouted that slave-owners had no rights. Southerners, especially after John Brown was hailed by most Northerners as a hero and a martyr, felt that there was no tie left between North and South, and that secession was the only way out. And so, here in the United States, emancipation had to be brought about only by a frightful war between North and South, some of the bad effects of which are still with us.

When, one day in 1862, Harriet Beecher Stowe came to call on President Lincoln at the White House, he greeted her with these words, "So this is the little woman who wrote the book which made this big war." In a special sense, he was right, for her book influenced hundreds of thousands who never would have listened to Abolition speeches. It was *Uncle Tom's Cabin* which alienated the South and convinced the North that in this land of liberty, where "all men are created equal," there is no place for human bondage. It was not long after Mrs. Stowe paid that call at the White House that Lincoln issued his Emancipation Proclamation, and the deed was done.

LOUIS BRAILLE

LOUIS BRAILLE

VI. LOUIS BRAILLE

January 4, 1809—January 6, 1852

In a village about forty miles east of Paris, there was born to a humble leather-worker named Braille and his wife, nearly a hundred and fifty years ago, a boy, the youngest of four children, whom the parents named Louis. The rough, stone house in which he first saw the light is still preserved as a memorial, but it isn't much of a dwelling by modern standards. It has only two rooms, one on the ground floor and one upstairs under the roof. The family lived on the ground floor, of course, but a part of that room was used by the father as his harness shop, so that there always was, mixed in with the cooking smells, the strong odor of leather. At night the family slept on pallets of straw laid on the floor. At best, that was not a very comfortable home, but little Louis knew nothing better, and his playmates probably had much the same kind of homes.

Shortly before his fourth birthday, the child was playing with a sharp knife on his father's work bench. Suddenly it flipped up and wounded one of his eyes which soon became blind. Unfortunately, as often happens, the other eye was infected, too, and soon poor little Louis was totally blind. But out of that dreadful affliction came the gift to all the blind everywhere which marks Louis Braille as one of the world's great humanitarians.

Blindness is still one of the most common misfortunes; some are born blind; others, like Louis Braille, are made sightless by accident; and still others grow sightless with disease or age. In Asia, for thousands of years, blind people were cast out of their homes as accursed. In some backward parts of Europe the blind were often rented out as beasts of burden, costing less than horses or oxen. Others were put to shoveling coal in factories or raking manure on farms all day long, and permitted to sleep on the ground at night as a special favor. For the most part, however, in both Asia and Europe, the blind were trained to be beggars, to whine on street corners or on the steps of temples and churches for a piece of bread or a copper coin. It was not so bad in the village of Coupvray where Louis lived. The neighbors were good to the little blind boy and tried to make life easier and pleasanter for him.

The local priest was especially kind, and if a member of the Braille family was unable to attend to it, there was always a playmate who would take Louis by the hand and lead him to school. For two years he attended this village school along with the boys who had their sight, and he surprised his teacher by the quickness with which he learned his lessons by ear and memory.

It happened that the schoolmaster had heard of a school for the young blind in Paris; and with Louis in mind, he mentioned the institution to the priest. The latter went to a rich and kindly nobleman named D'Orvilliers, who lived near by in his ancestral manor house, to ask help in getting Louis accepted. Now it happened that D'Orvilliers remembered meeting the man who had founded that school for the blind, Valentin Haüy, and had encouraged him to go ahead with his plan by contributing a large sum of money toward the enterprise. At once the nobleman wrote to the director of the school, asking him to accept Louis Braille, and naturally that request was granted. In this way the first door of opportunity was opened.

At the time he was admitted, in February, 1819, Louis was just ten years old. Naturally, at first he was homesick, but that feeling soon wore off, and he learned to be happy in his new surroundings. And from the first he distinguished himself as a brilliant student. He showed a talent for music, too, and was encouraged to learn to play the piano. Later he turned to the organ and became a skilled church organist in his early manhood. Fortunately, the teachers, from the director down, encouraged him in every way. Louis Braille was destined to be connected with this school for the rest of his life, first as pupil and then as teacher.

Naturally, the great problem in teaching the blind was to devise some way in which they could learn to read without eyes. Valentin Haüy, the philanthropist who founded this Institute for the Young Blind, had invented raised or embossed type, letters that a blind person could make out by feeling them with his fingertips. This was an important beginning, but the process was difficult and expensive, and the letters had to be printed so big in order to be recognized with the fingers that a small book in ordinary type would require several volumes in embossed type. Also, while it was possible to feel out a word, letter by letter, it made reading very slow.

In June of the same year in which Louis entered the Institute, an artillery captain named Charles Barbier wrote to the Academy of Sciences in Paris, to say that he had invented a method of sending messages by means of dots and dashes "in relief"; that is, standing above the surface like embossed type. These dots and dashes, grouped in different ways, could stand for military orders or messages, such as "retreat to the main line," "enemy is on your right," etc., and a sentry or outpost could receive the word at night without the necessity of striking a light, which would betray the position to the enemy. Captain Barbier used cardboard or thick paper and punched these dots and dashes by using a tool pressed on the back of the sheet. He called this invention night-writing, or Sonography, and he suggested that it deserved the attention of the men of science. The Academy appointed two of their members to investigate and make a report. They said that what they thought most important about this night-writing was that it might help the blind to read.

Hearing this, Captain Barbier called on the officials of the Institute for the Young Blind and showed them his system of communicating in the dark. But they weren't interested. The head of the Institution was soon afterward dismissed from his post and another man became director. The officer returned to see what he could do with the new man. This visit left a deeper impression, because soon afterward the director called the whole school together—teachers and pupils—to let them try out this new device. When Louis Braille felt the little lumps of cardboard under his fingers, he was overjoyed. Here, the boy realized, was the key to what the blind needed more than anything else!

True enough, as Louis realized when he began experimenting by himself, this system of writing was clumsy and complicated, but all the same he felt that in some form or other this was important. What the system needed was cutting, revision and general improvement to make it practicable for the blind, and to that task Louis Braille dedicated the rest of his life.

Except for his beloved music, all his energy was concentrated on this problem of making night-writing really useful for the blind, of making up an easy-to-read alphabet by means of raised dots. He spent long night hours on this work when he should have been sleeping, and often his comrades found him in the morning asleep over his piece of cardboard and punching tool. The other pupils and the teachers didn't laugh at him because they were all interested. In fact, the director wrote to Captain Barbier that his Sonography would be used at the Institute as "an auxiliary method of teaching."

At this time it should be remembered that Louis Braille was only fifteen years old. It is truly remarkable that this invention was being worked on constantly and most intelligently by a pupil at the school who was only a lad when he began. For the more Louis labored over the Barbier system, the more he discovered its practical drawbacks for the blind. And in the Barbier code there was no provision for such things as punctuation, accents, figures or musical notes.

When Captain Barbier learned that a pupil at the school was making improvements in Sonography, he came to see. To his astonishment he found it was a fifteen-year-old boy. Barbier himself was then fifty-five. On being asked about the work, Louis explained the improvements that the system needed, but it was more than the veteran officer could stand to hear criticisms of his system from a mere boy, and he went away in a huff. Louis was sorry to have offended him, but he knew that the drawbacks in the code were very real for blind people, a fact that the officer, not being blind himself, could not realize.

Fortunately, Louis was not in the least discouraged. During the summer vacation in his home village of Coupvray, he would sit out under the trees, day after day, and punch away, aiming at perfection in an alphabet for the blind. And it should be added that when he went back to school he did not let his deep interest in this project interfere with his studies. He won prizes for scholarship and made steady progress in his lessons on the piano. He was good

Louis Braille

at shop work, too. When he was only fourteen he had been appointed foreman for the workshop where slippers were being made by the pupils. He excelled in every aspect of the school life.

This fact was recognized officially, when in the year 1826, he was appointed to help in the teaching, taking classes in algebra, grammar and geography, and was asked to give piano lessons to beginners. He was then only seventeen. At the same time Louis was carrying on his own studies. He even took courses at the College de France. In music, he branched out from piano to organ and made himself a skilled performer on that instrument as well.

All the while, however, his main interest lay in the new writing code, and he made no secret of it. He gave a brilliant demonstration to one of the senior members of the teaching staff, and explained it to the other pupils. They were all enthusiastic, but Louis was not satisfied. He wanted perfection. Having made up his alphabet, he wanted to make the little raised dots represent musical notes, too, so that a blind musician like himself could learn to play a score just by his fingertips. By the time he was nineteen he had accomplished this also. He wrote music in seven octaves, and indicated each octave by a special symbol. The following year he published a small book on this way of writing music for the blind, and in this he gave full credit to the artillery officer, Captain Barbier, for the original idea of raised dots as symbols for finger reading.

Meanwhile, in 1828, Louis had been appointed assistant instructor at the Institute. His salary was fifteen francs a month—only three dollars, if we reckon the franc at its old value of twenty cents—but he lived at the school and was very happy in his work. He had been chosen for the teaching job when he was nineteen, not only because he had made good in every side of the life and work of the school but because he had a warm, friendly personality. He was popular with the boys and equally so with the teachers. And the head of the school felt that the work this youth was doing on an alphabet for the blind might turn out to be of great importance.

As a full-time teacher Louis was strikingly successful because he was so beloved by his pupils that they would do anything for him, and he was always thinking up ways of making the subjects he taught interesting. One of his students, many years afterward, wrote these words about the young instructor:

"He carried out his duties with so much charm and wisdom that the obligation of attending class was transformed into a real pleasure for his pupils. They competed not only to equal and surpass each other but also in a moving and constant effort to please a teacher whom they admired as a superior and liked as a wise and well-informed friend, ready with sound advice."

By the time Louis Braille was twenty-four, he was so far advanced in his organ studies that he was appointed organist at the Church of Notre Dame des Champs in Paris; this, despite his blindness. He loved this side of his life not only because of his passion for music but because of his religious nature, his deep-rooted faith, unshaken by his affliction.

That faith was soon doomed to withstand another test still more severe. When he was only twenty-six, he was stricken with tuberculosis, a disease which in that year, 1835, had no cure in medicine. From that time, except for occasional brief periods of betterment, Louis's health steadily went downhill. In 1840, such was his reputation as a teacher of the blind that he was offered the post of teacher to a blind prince of the royal family of Austria. But the long journey to Vienna would have been too great a strain on Louis's waning strength, and he had to decline. He continued to teach at the Institute, however, until 1844, when the director relieved him of his classes on account of his physical condition. At the same time he had to give up his post as organist at the church, but he saw to it that someone else obtained it who needed the job.

Three years later there was a flash of improvement in Louis's health and he was allowed to try part-time teaching again; but this was no permanent improvement, though he continued, after a fashion, for four years more as one of the teachers at the Institute. At the end of that time he had to give up again, and by the close of the year 1851 he had taken to his bed, never to rise again. On January 6, 1852, he died, and was buried in the little cemetery at Coupvray.

As his life drew to a close, Louis Braille had the discouragement of know-

Louis Braille

ing that the work to which he had devoted the best thought of his life, from the time he was fifteen years old, had not been truly appreciated or accepted anywhere, outside of the little experimenting that had gone on at his own school. His death was unnoticed by the public. However, he was so beloved at the Institute that the very next year a portrait bust was unveiled there; and, not long after, his system of writing and printing for the blind was formally accepted. Gradually that system spread, as its advantages became known. In 1887 a national monument was set up in the market place at Coupvray, now called "Le Place Braille." On one side of the pedestal is the Braille alphabet, and on another is a carving showing Braille teaching a blind child. On top is a portrait bust.

Since then the Braille system has won acceptance all over the world, in all languages. It is true, as he was the first to admit, that he got the original idea from Captain Barbier, but the latter's system was far too clumsy and too limited. Braille cut Barbier's letter space—called a "cell"—by one-half, creating a cell that is three dots high and two dots wide, something much easier for the finger to trace. In this he arranged the dots into combinations which represent letters of the alphabet, marks of punctuation, numerals, capitals and musical notes, going far beyond anything that Captain Barbier had ever dreamed of.

For writing in Braille there is a slate and a punching tool called a stylus. The slate is a smooth board over which is fitted a metal frame, with its surface grooved to make the spaces for the letters. Each space or cell is perforated with six holes. A sheet of specially prepared thick paper is laid on the board; then the dots are made by punching with the stylus through the holes in the metal frame. The writing is from right to left, because the paper has to be turned over to be read.

Since this invention opened to the blind the world of literature, science, history, and even music, Louis Braille has been well described as "one of the great benefactors of the world." On June 22, 1952, over a hundred years after his death, an impressive scene took place in Paris. A long procession of blind people, each carrying his white cane, marched slowly toward a famous building called the Pantheon, where lie the remains of France's honored dead. This column of the blind followed the coffin of Louis Braille, which had been removed from the village cemetery in order that it might lie in the most honorable resting place that the nation could offer. Immediately behind the coffin marched members of the Braille family, and then the professors and students of the Institute for the Young Blind. A military band played funeral marches, and all along the route the church bells rang.

This ceremonial came a hundred years late, but it did serve to give public recognition to a man who, although unappreciated in his own lifetime, nevertheless gave all he had, despite a long and fatal illness, in order to help those whom he called his brothers to overcome their handicap of darkness and to help them to live useful and happy lives. No other man in history has ever accomplished so much for the blind as Louis Braille.

FLORENCE NIGHTINGALE

FLORENCE NIGHTINGALE

VII. FLORENCE NIGHTINGALE

May 12, 1820—August 3, 1910

As Joan of Arc is the national heroine of France, Florence Nightingale is the national heroine of Britain. Both women won their fame in wars, but in different ways. The Frenchwoman led armies to victory; the Englishwoman cared for the sick and wounded soldiers that victories left behind. But, as we shall see, she did more; she became the patron saint of all nurses the world over, because she made nursing an honorable profession for women instead of the degraded occupation that it was in her own day.

Florence was one of two daughters born into the family of an English country gentleman. Her parents were socially prominent as well as wealthy. The father served for forty years in Parliament, where he made a record of backing such good causes as religious freedom and protection for the aged, the sick and the destitute. The mother, too, had a kind heart, and even as a child Florence used to accompany her when she would go out with a basket on her arm filled with good things for the old and the sick among the tenants on the estate. And so it can be said that Florence was brought up with the idea of consideration for the less fortunate in life.

But it may be interesting at this point to note how she came by the name Florence. Like other well-to-do English couples of their day, the Nightingales often traveled on the Continent. It was during the first of these journeys that their first daughter was born in Naples. Mr. Nightingale decided that it would be appropriate to name her after the early Greek settlement on the site of that city, "Parthenope." It was an odd name for an English girl, but it was soon shortened in general use to "Parthe."

Famous Humanitarians

On another trip to Italy, the second daughter was born. Her birthplace happened to be Florence. So, to be consistent, Mr. Nightingale named the child Florence. Probably no other girl was ever saddled with the name Parthenope, but such was the luster that Florence Nightingale shed on her name that Florence has long since been one of the most popular names for girls among English-speaking peoples. So it is interesting to remember that the first girl to bear that name was the subject of this sketch.

Because Florence was born an aristocrat, she was expected to follow the path laid down for other girls of her class. This meant an ornamental education by governesses, followed by presentation at Court, as a debut into society. After that there would be a round of parties and visits, interspersed with trips to the Continent, and finally a brilliant marriage. Florence had good looks, an attractive personality and a fine mind. Her mother counted on her becoming a famous belle, "and, perhaps, who knows? She may even marry a peer!" Parthe, for her part, accepted this life without a question; and, after all, in those days what else could a well-born English girl do?

But these plans did not take into account Florence herself. She soon showed that she was bored with parties and small talk. She had her own ideas of what she wanted to do with her life, and that, in the first half of the nineteenth century, was positively shocking. Her desire to be something more than a mere society woman, to make her life a service to humanity seems to have been crystallized in her heart by something mysterious that happened when she was only sixteen. "On February 7, 1837," she wrote in her diary, "God spoke to me and called me to His service." She described this as a voice that she heard clearly, speaking to her when she was alone and wide awake. However one may try to explain it, she herself believed it to be a Divine call. And this mystic experience is all the more remarkable because Florence was never given to imagining things. No other woman of the Victorian era proved to be so hard-headed and practical as she. In later years she left a note saying that at three other crises in her life—as, for example, just before she sailed for the Crimea—she heard that voice again, speaking to her. Certainly it was very real to her, and we may remember that Joan of Arc also heard voices. She, too, never doubted them, and though only a peasant girl she obeyed and led

Florence Nightingale

armies to victory. At any rate, from the day that Florence Nightingale first heard that call to service as a girl of sixteen, she never flinched from her resolve to make her life one of service to God and man.

From the first, her interest was attracted to the idea of bettering hospital conditions and of lifting the degraded profession of nursing. On her travels she was much more interested in hospitals abroad than in cathedrals and galleries. "What has got into you, Florence?" her mother would ask, and the answer was never satisfactory. Why should a nice girl be interested in nursing? At that time the only nurses in England were a disgraceful lot of women of low character, drawn from the slums, and notorious for drunkenness. Of course, these creatures had no medical training whatever, being merely human dregs that were willing to do the most menial and unpleasant work. It seems strange to us now that British doctors were satisfied with such nurses. But they had never known anything better. To Florence, the situation was a scandal. Something had to be done.

After thinking a great deal about the subject, she stated that she herself would like to be a nurse, a real nurse with medical training. Also, she would like to set up a training school for other women to become nurses. At this suggestion her mother and Parthe nearly fainted away. Imagine a girl of high birth and breeding wanting to be—of all things—a nurse! They would not have been more shocked if Florence had said, "I'd like to be a barmaid."

On returning from a journey abroad in 1839, Florence had to submit to being presented at Court and making her formal debut in society. Her mother hoped that the gaiety and glitter would put this nursing nonsense out of Florence's mind. But it didn't work out that way. Florence just wouldn't be a social butterfly.

In 1844, during this period of restless boredom, an American doctor, Samuel Gridley Howe, and his wife, were invited to visit the Nightingales. After a romantic career with the Greeks fighting for their independence, Dr. Howe had gone home to Boston, and later had been asked to head up a new institution for the blind in Boston. He accepted and soon made an international reputation. Probably it was Mr. Nightingale's interest in good causes that prompted the invitation. Florence managed to get Dr. Howe alone for a quiet talk, the morning after his arrival.

"Will you answer a question frankly?" she asked.

"I shall be delighted."

"If I should decide to study nursing and devote the rest of my life to nursing, do you think it would be a dreadful thing?"

"No, not dreadful but unusual. In England," he added with a smile, "whatever is unusual is considered unfitting."

"Yes, I know. Everyone tells me that, but I am sure that nursing is my vocation."

"Then you must go on with it without fear, wherever it may lead you, and God be with you."

Florence's face shone with a new light of happiness. This stranger—this American—understood, giving her the first and only word of encouragement she had ever received. It is interesting to remember that this American doctor, who himself became one of the world's great humanitarians because of his work for the blind, was the person who, when Florence Nightingale most needed sympathy and encouragement, gave it to her.

As she reflected on the problem later, she decided that the best way to achieve her ambition would be to organize a sort of sisterhood of trained nurses. In her travels she had studied the Catholic Sisters of Saint Vincent de Paul in Paris, and had spent three months as one of the Lutheran Pastor Fliedner's student "Deaconesses" in a training school for nursing at Kaiserswoth on the Rhine.

In 1853, while she was still making plans for starting a nursing school in England, she was offered the superintendency of a London hospital called "The Establishment for Gentlewomen During Illness." She had been named for this position by a lifelong friend, Sidney Herbert, who saw in this job an opening for Florence to begin her work. She accepted, but found that the management of the institution was in the hands of a committee of socially prominent women, who from the first frowned on Florence as a young lady with queer ideas. Privately she called them "The Society of Fashionable Asses." This was her first schooling in overcoming opposition single-handed.

Florence Nightingale

Wonderful to relate, she won her battle every time, for she was a person of iron will, and it happened that she was always right.

In that very year, 1853, Turkey declared war on Russia. And in the following year, France and Britain joined in as Turkey's allies in what history calls the Crimean War. The first great battle, Alma, took place in September, and although it was an allied victory, it involved terrible losses. A war correspondent named Russell sent dispatches to the London *Times*, giving a horrifying picture of the aftermath of that battle. He said that there were not nearly enough surgeons, no nurses at all, and not even linen for bandages. "The French have their Sisters of Mercy," he wrote, "why is it that we British have no nurses whatever?"

The British public was furious, as more and more shocking details came from Russell's pen, especially the picture he gave of the state of the British military hospital in Scutari, a suburb of Constantinople. To Florence Nightingale it seemed a call for her. Although as yet she had no corps of trained nurses, she must go herself with such women as might serve well under her direction. There was no time to lose, for soldiers were dying by the thousands from neglect. She wrote to the wife of her friend Sidney Herbert, who then was an important man in the Government, offering her services. At the very time she was writing, he himself was penning a letter to her, suggesting that this was her great opportunity. Since the two letters crossed, there was no time lost in obtaining permission. Also, she was given sole authority to handle the plan of getting a group of nurses to Scutari. "You will find the task full of horrors and hardships," wrote Herbert, but he could not realize how dreadfully true those words would prove to be.

It was no easy task to find women with any qualifications for nursing. But she finally mustered thirty-eight, most of them either members of a Catholic or an Episcopalian sisterhood. On October 21, 1854, she and her band of nurses set sail from London. They brought with them many things that the war correspondent had reported were desperately needed by the sick and wounded, such as blankets, medicines, hospital food and linen for bandages, bought partly by Florence Nightingale's own money and partly by the contributions of English citizens.

Famous Humanitarians

It was a slow, seasick voyage before the Nightingale mission set foot on land again, heading for that military hospital at Scutari. On arrival, these women had to walk in a cold rain a half mile up a steep road to the hospital. One would think that the military authorities, knowing when the nurses would arrive, might have sent carriages to convey them to their goal. But the army authorities, especially the medical people, were wild with rage because they declared, "our troops lack for nothing." Among the big lies of history, this one could claim a first prize. What these little men resented was the fact that their inefficiency was being shown up. And who was this Miss Nightingale to come meddling in the affairs of the British Army?

So the nurses, with Florence Nightingale at their head, marched up the hill to the so-called hospital. Never has a band of crusaders had such a reception. As they entered the courtyard, they stopped with a gasp of horror. The whole area was a mass of muck and filth, strewn with amputated arms and legs. And in the midst of these lay a dead mule!

Then and there, Miss Nightingale gave her first order. Seeing a British soldier, she called out, "This courtyard must be cleaned immediately!"

It seems unbelievable now that the officers in charge could have permitted such a state of things. But, as it was proved later, the surgeons did their amputations in the corridors of the building and tossed legs and arms out of the windows. It was called a hospital, but it was soon all too evident that the war correspondent, Russell, had not exaggerated the horrors of the place. Florence Nightingale discovered that the building had originally been a Turkish barracks and had been turned over to the British to use as a hospital. All that had been done to it was to give it a coat of whitewash. There was not one piece of hospital equipment, and practically no plumbing. The whole building reeked with stench, the woodwork was alive with vermin, and rats scurried along the walls. Men with contagious diseases were laid alongside the uninfected. Hardly had the Nightingale party arrived when a new batch of wounded men, who had been on a week-long voyage across the Black Sea from Balaclava, were being carried in. They had had no medical care on the ship. No one will ever know how many died from neglect on that voyage. And those that were still alive were brought in wearing their uniforms caked with

Florence Nightingale

mud and stiff with their own blood. There were no clean clothes for them at Scutari; there weren't even beds for them, so they had to be laid on the floor.

Such was the problem that Florence Nightingale had to face and solve somehow. Each new battle meant another wave of wounded men filling the available space so closely that eighteen inches between the patients was all that could be spared for doctors and nurses to pass. How those nurses, and especially their leader, managed to stand up under the strain of these conditions is almost a miracle. And all the while Florence Nightingale had to fight against the red tape of army regulations and the jealousy of ranking medical officers. Why should anyone take all this interest in common soldiers, anyway? "You'll spoil the brutes," was the way one ranking official put it to her. And they all thought it funny to refer to her as "The Bird."

It is a long, heroic story of overcoming obstacles, but steadily she and her nurses made things better. Fortunately, she had the people back home heart and soul with her. And the gratitude of the men themselves was beyond words. It is said that, as she walked through the wards for her late night inspection, carrying a lamp, the men who were able to turn on their mattresses would kiss her shadow as it fell upon the wall. It is because of this custom of hers to make a final personal inspection of the whole hospital every night that she earned her famous title, "The Lady with the Lamp."

After a terrible winter at Scutari, Florence Nightingale decided that she must visit the field hospitals in the fighting area. Accordingly, she took ship across the Black Sea to Balaclava. While on this tour she visited the front lines. When the men in the trenches found out who she was, they cheered so loudly that the Russians in Sebastopol heard them and asked each other what had happened to the British army. Although ranking medical officers had referred to her as a "meddling fool," Lord Raglan, the Commander-in-Chief, appreciated her magnificent services to his men and gave her every courtesy. Unfortunately, on this tour she fell a victim to what was called "Crimean Fever." She collapsed and had to be carried to bed. Although it was a contagious disease, Lord Raglan came to her bedside and gave her every attention in his power. She was desperately ill but took a turn for the better and finally recovered.

In November she received a warm letter of appreciation from the Queen, with a gift of a brooch set with jewels. It was engraved, "To Miss Florence Nightingale as a mark of esteem and gratitude for her devotion to the Queen's brave soldiers. From Victoria R. 1855."

In that year the war ended and all hospitals became empty as the men were shipped home. Florence Nightingale's work in the war was done. The British government offered her passage back on a man of war, and the people of England clamored for a big public reception. But she declined both with thanks, and arrived home as an ordinary passenger under the name of "Miss Smith."

Her most spectacular work was done in that war. But in the many years left of her life she gave herself up to one reform after another, with hard work and dull, despite constant ill health. Perhaps her greatest achievement in the post-war years was the founding of a Nightingale Training School for Nurses. With this she realized at last her lifelong ambition, and that institution—soon copied everywhere in the civilized world—put nursing where it belonged as a noble and a skilled profession.

Her interest in the army never slackened, especially her determination to improve the lot of the common soldier, about whom nobody had ever cared before. Thanks to her, a great change for the better took place in the army medical organization and practice.

Many honors were showered upon her, and she received many tributes from other lands, as for instance Longfellow's poem, "The Lady with the Lamp." When a Crimean War monument was erected in London, one of the figures was a portrait statue of her, the first statue ever erected in Britain to any woman not a member of royalty.

When the end came on August 3, 1910, she was ninety years old and quite blind, but still venerated by the entire civilized world. There was a popular demand that she be buried in Westminster Abbey, but her family said no; it had been her desire to be laid beside her parents in the parish churchyard. However, as a last tribute from the army, six stalwart sergeants received the honor of carrying her coffin, and over it, as for a military hero, was spread her country's flag.

JEAN HENRI DUNANT
CLARA HARLOWE BARTON

JEAN HENRI DUNANT

CLARA BARTON

VIII. JEAN HENRI DUNANT

May 8, 1828—October 30, 1910

CLARA HARLOWE BARTON

December 25, 1821—April 12, 1912

IN THE YEAR 1859 there was living in Geneva, Switzerland, a fine-looking young man who, at the age of thirty-one, was already known in the city as a successful banker and a warm-hearted philanthropist. In fact, his parents and grandparents had made names for themselves as well-to-do citizens who never forgot the sick and the needy among their fellow-townsmen, and when Jean Henri Dunant grew up he determined to carry on that fine tradition of helping those in distress.

One day in early June, 1859, Henri Dunant—he preferred Henri to Jean— set out in his coach for a journey to north Italy. In that very year a war broke out. The King of Sardinia, helped by Napoleon III of France, was making a desperate effort to free Italy from the yoke of Austria, which in those days ruled all the way to the Alps, except for Rome, which was under the Pope. It did not look like a very appropriate time to visit Italy, but Henri Dunant was sure that he could manage to keep out of the way of the two armies, and off he rattled in his coach, looking forward to an interesting and pleasant vacation.

By the time he had crossed the Alps and had entered Italy, one terrible battle had already been fought, named after a near-by town, Magenta. It was so bloody that ever since then the name magenta has been given to a certain shade of red. The two armies met again at a place near the city of Solferino, not far from Brescia in Northern Italy. And, just as the battle was joined, Henri Dunant arrived on the scene in his coach. What he saw that day and the following days so wrung his heart that he not only worked tirelessly himself, night and day, caring for the wounded, but when he returned home he wrote a little book, *A Memory of Solferino*, which made a sensation. That book is almost completely forgotten now, as is also the name of the man who wrote it. But out of those pages sprang a magnificent organization for helping mankind, the International Red Cross.

The conditions that Dunant witnessed at Solferino immediately after the battle were so horrible that most of them must be left to the imagination. But a brief picture of the battle and its aftermath is necessary to our story. After Magenta the Austrian army had retreated. Neither side knew where the other was until at daybreak on June 24, 1859 they clashed unexpectedly. The Austrians had been marching all night and came to the battle exhausted, without food or water. The French were served coffee before dawn, but neither army had any food or water during the entire day-long battle. As the sun rose, the heat became intense, adding to the sufferings of the men on both sides. Then a wind arose, sweeping great clouds of choking dust over the battlefield.

The fighting began at 3 A.M. By six o'clock all the troops were engaged, 300,000 men. Much of the fighting was hand-to-hand with bayonets. Then the cavalry charged over the bodies lying on the ground, both dead and wounded. At five in the afternoon, a great storm of wind, rain and lightning burst over the field, putting an end to the conflict. Under cover of that storm the Austrians retreated, and the battle of Solferino was over. Practically all the Austrian wounded were left behind, lying where they had fallen. When night came, French and Sardinian soldiers roamed the battlefield looking for missing comrades amid the silent dead and the screaming, helpless wounded.

At the opening of the battle, so-called field hospitals were set up in farmhouses, churches, barns, and open spaces under the trees. Some doctors had been brought with the French army, but far too few. Those surgeons made amputations and dressed wounds until they collapsed from exhaustion. What they were able to do barely touched the needs, because when night fell on Solferino, 40,000 men lay on the field, dead or wounded. There was no water for the wounded except the muddy puddles made by the thunderstorm, and even this was tainted with the blood of men and horses.

The French army was supposed to have a quartermaster's department equipped to care for wounded men, but this was so hopelessly inadequate that untold thousands died from mere neglect, a great many bleeding to death from unbandaged wounds. Moreover, there was not nearly enough chloroform to use in amputations, no proper ambulances for transferring the wounded to field hospitals, nothing but springless carts and donkeys with chairs strapped to their sides. Many of the wounded had to lie where they had fallen for two to three days.

All this dreadful scene was spread before the shocked eyes of the young Swiss tourist. He was not the sort of man to say "Isn't this awful?" and walk back to his coach. At once he became a volunteer worker, and he gathered men and women from neighboring farms and villages to help. All that night after the battle he toiled, his heart torn by the terrible suffering all around him. Then he followed the procession of wounded to the neighboring city of Castiglione, which was soon so jammed with the unfortunates that many were laid on straw in public squares, with only a bit of canvas rigged to keep the sun off their faces. Dunant described this town as "one vast hospital," but a hospital would have had a staff of surgeons, nurses and orderlies, and here there was only a handful of doctors, and no other trained personnel. In this terrible picture of suffering there was only one redeeming feature—that, among the workers, there was no distinction made between friend and foe. The motto in Italian was "Tutti fratelli," meaning "all are brothers."

It was soon after Dunant returned home that he wrote his book, *A Memory of Solferino*. In this he proposed an international organization to care for the sick and wounded soldiers in all wars.

"Why have I told you all these scenes of pain and distress?" he wrote. "Would it not be possible in time of peace and quiet to form relief societies for the purpose of having care given to the wounded in wartime by zealous, devoted and thoroughly qualified volunteers? If an international relief society had existed at the time of Solferino . . . what endless suffering it could have prevented!"

With this little book, Dunant started a one-man crusade to create just such an international relief society. To this end he spent his own time and money lavishly. Fortunately, he was helped in this crusade by the head of the Swiss army, General Dufour, a man of great influence. These men succeeded in calling an international conference, meeting in Geneva, attended by delegates from fourteen nations. These delegates drew up an agreement still known as "The Geneva Convention." In honor of the young Swiss who had started the movement, the convention adopted as the sacred flag of the relief organization the design of the Swiss flag, except that the colors were reversed. Instead of a white cross on a red ground, the new flag consisted of a red cross on a white ground. Ever since, the organization has gone by the name of the Red Cross.

Originally planned only for the relief of the sick and wounded soldiers in war, it has since spread out to all areas of suffering. But the international headquarters are still at Geneva, happily the capital of a country that has been neutral in every modern war.

Meanwhile, the author of this noble undertaking, Henri Dunant, had given so much time and money to the cause that in 1867 he went bankrupt. Unfortunately, some of his friends lost their investments through his failure in business. Feeling disgraced before the world, he left Geneva for Paris, where he let himself become lost and forgotten, except for a brief time when the Franco-Prussian War broke out in 1870. When that ended, he disappeared again and it was not until twenty years later that he was rediscovered by a Swiss schoolteacher, living in an old men's home in Switzerland. At that time Dunant was sixty-two. Everyone had thought that he must have been long since dead. The schoolteacher took Dunant into his own home and treated him with great kindness. For a while he became active again in the Red Cross. But failing health sent him back to the old men's home. There the white-bearded patriarch lived once more unnoticed and forgotten for another eighteen years.

At the end of that time a Swiss newspaper man rediscovered Dunant, then very old, sick and poor. But his work had not been forgotten, and he shared with a man named Frederic Passy the first Nobel Peace Prize. It was charac-

Clara Harlowe Barton

teristic of Henri Dunant that, in spite of his old age, poverty and feeble health, he gave all of his share of that prize money to charities. Nine years later, on an October day, he died, feeling, no doubt, that his life had been a failure. But, judged by what he succeeded in creating, what life could have been more successful? Of *A Memory of Solferino*, a biographer says, "Few books have equalled this small volume as an instrument of prompt, effective and far-reaching benefit to humanity."

Clara Harlowe Barton

In the United States, the name Red Cross is closely linked with an American woman, Clara Barton, still honored as one of the heroines in our nation's history. During the Civil War years, 1861-1865, she earned for herself from the lips of Union soldiers the title of "The Angel of the Battlefields," for she moved about among the wounded even while the bullets were still flying. But she began her nursing long before, when she was only eleven years old. It happened that her daredevil brother David, while doing a climbing stunt on the barn, fell from the roof and suffered serious injuries. For months he hovered between life and death, and in all that time she devoted herself to nursing him. And he wanted no one but her. For two whole years she tried to make David well again. She gave up her friends, her play, her outdoors, and her schooling in order to nurse her brother. It is said that no one else in the family was as skillful as she, the "little sister Clara."

As she grew up she went into teaching, which was almost the only profession a woman could enter in those days. She wasn't just another "Yankee schoolmarm." When the family moved from Massachusetts to Bordentown, New Jersey, she found out that, on account of some squabble among the town politicians, the children of the poor were running wild because their parents could not pay for private schools. Clara got hold of an unused building and began a school of her own. When she started she had six pupils; when she had to stop, completely exhausted, with her voice gone, she was teaching six hundred! From 1855 to 1861 she took a job as government clerk in Washington.

Then came the firing on Sumter. When the Sixth Massachusetts regiment marched through Baltimore, the men were stoned by a mob of Southern sympathizers, and the soldiers arrived in Washington bruised and wounded, with all their baggage gone. And there were no supplies for them at the capital. Although she was only a government clerk, Clara put an advertisement in a Washington paper, asking for contributions for the soldiers, and then she opened an agency to handle the gifts.

From this service she went on to more and greater tasks. After the Battle of Bull Run, she realized that many lives could have been saved—as at Solferino—if there had been first aid on the battlefield. At that time no women were allowed near the front, but Clara Barton knew that the army needed nothing so desperately as a corps of trained nurses. She managed to plead her cause so eloquently that soon she was given permission to serve at the front, her first battle experience being at Antietam. Her contempt for danger is illustrated by one incident on the field. She was giving a drink of water to a wounded soldier when a Confederate bullet cut through her skirt and killed the man.

Again, at the terrible battle of Fredericksburg, she was a ministering angel to the stricken men. In this fearful defeat for the Union army, many of the helpless wounded actually froze to death in the snow before they could be rescued. But how many lives were saved by Clara Barton it would be impossible to estimate. She seemed to be everywhere, getting the wounded onto the trains to be taken to base hospitals, cooking hot gruel, washing and bandaging wounds, and bringing water. Once a fragment of shell tore through her dress, but again she escaped harm.

These scenes were typical of the service that made her the Angel of the Battlefields. After the war she performed another great service. She established a bureau for locating the soldiers reported as missing. The work that she accomplished with this bureau won for her the devout gratitude of countless fathers and mothers.

All this meant a great strain on her frail little body, and the doctors sent her to Switzerland to rest. It was there that for the first time she learned of the International Red Cross, and she discovered, too, that the United States government, all absorbed in its own great war, had never joined. Soon the Franco-Prussian War broke out. The Grand Duchess of Baden drove up to her door to beg her to help in this war as she had done in the American war. Although she was still weak, she responded, and organized at Strasbourg and at Paris a great relief work. After the war she was awarded the Gold Cross of Baden, the Iron Cross of Germany, and Queen Victoria, with her own hands, pinned a British decoration on her dress. Again Clara broke down from overwork and was an invalid for years thereafter.

In 1884 she was able to accept the appointment as American representative at the Red Cross Conference and the International Peace Convention in Geneva. While there, she made the suggestion which greatly broadened the work of the Red Cross. Henri Dunant's plea had been in behalf of the wounded and the sick soldiers in time of war. Clara Barton said, "Let's spread our mission of mercy to every place where there is calamity and distress in peace time as well as war." The idea caught hold and, beginning with a typhus epidemic in the Black Sea region, the Red Cross has since spread its healing and rescue work to all areas of suffering, such as were caused by earthquake, hurricane, fire, and flood.

Clara Barton was appointed by Congress the first President of the American Red Cross and she held that post until 1904. At the age of seventy-nine she actively managed the relief work for the victims of the great Galveston flood disaster. Fortunately, in spite of her many breakdowns from overwork, Clara Barton lived to see the wonderful development of her inspired idea of the Red Cross serving in peace as well as in war, for she lived to be nearly ninety-one.

We know now that such terrible scenes as were witnessed by Henri Dunant at Solferino, and Clara Barton at Fredericksburg, shall never be witnessed again, thanks to the Red Cross. And when a great disaster comes in time of peace, we know, too, that the Red Cross will fly to the scene with nurses, doctors, food, clothing and medicine. For this great service to humanity we must all remember, with deep and humble gratitude, this man and this woman, who gave their all to make the Red Cross ideal of mercy to mankind come true.

WILLIAM BOOTH
EVANGELINE CORY BOOTH

WILLIAM BOOTH

EVANGELINE BOOTH

IX. WILLIAM BOOTH

April 10, 1829—August 20, 1912

EVANGELINE CORY BOOTH

December 25, 1865—July 12, 1950

Everyone is familiar with the soldiers of the Salvation Army. At the Christmas season we see and hear them at street corners, in Santa Claus costume, jingling their bells and asking for contributions for the Christmas dinners the Army gives to the hungry. Every doughboy who served in World War I remembers with gratitude what the men and women of the Salvation Army did during that war for our men at the front. All through the years since it was first organized in 1865, its record has been a shining one, of countless lives saved from debauchery and crime, and of others rescued from misery and starvation. The Army's inspiring motto has been, "A man may be down but he is never out."

The two names at the head of this chapter are famous: the one as the founder of the Salvation Army; and the other, as his daughter whose whole life was spent in that army and who was specially noted for her work as head of the organization in the United States until her death.

In order to appreciate the services of the Salvation Army and the Booths, it is worth while to review briefly the conditions in England when William Booth began his work among the poor. It is now hard to believe that the Britain of Queen Victoria could ever have permitted such miseries and such abuses as were common then among what were called "the lower classes." And it is interesting to note that the first man to protest against these abuses was not himself one of the downtrodden masses, but an English peer, a member of the top aristocracy. He was Anthony Ashley Cooper, Lord Ashley, until the death of his father. Then he inherited the title by which he is now best known, the Earl of Shaftesbury.

First, he attacked the brutal way in which the insane were still being treated and brought about a reform of the lunacy laws, the same great work of mercy which an American woman, Dorothea Lynde Dix, was performing somewhat later for her own country. From this work for the insane, Shaftesbury turned to the factories. There he found horrible conditions. Children, for example, were being made to work ten hours a day. In one factory he saw a man going around with a watering pot of cold water, which he sprinkled on the heads of some of the children. The explanation given was that the youngsters often got so tired and drowsy tending their machines that they would fall asleep on their feet and fall into the machinery. That, of course, would be likely to injure the machines!

When Shaftesbury turned his attention to the coal mines, he found women and children working deep in the pits. In one mine he saw women hitched to cars bringing coal to the surface because women were cheaper than mules! The reports that he made to Parliament on factories and mines make horrifying reading today. He worked, too, on conditions in the slums, especially the dreadful life of the poor boys who were chimney sweeps in London. But he was unable to accomplish as much for the slum dwellers as he finally achieved for the workers in factories and mines. And it was as a force to raise the life of the city slums that the Salvation Army came into being.

William Booth was born, not in London, but in a suburb of Nottingham, a city which we associate with the story of Robin Hood. Here, William was sent to school, but the Booth fortunes fell so low that at thirteen the boy had to be taken out of school and apprenticed to a pawn-broker, a job that he always hated, yet did well. When he was fifteen, religion suddenly came to mean everything to him in life; he became, as the saying is, converted. More and more he grew indignant over the ragged and hungry children in

William Booth

the streets and the helpless old people begging for a scrap of bread, the misery all about him, which he felt Christians should never permit to exist. But in those days the churches were not active in social reforms. The respectable, well-to-do church folk seemed to feel that the poor should "learn to be content with the station to which God had called them." This attitude, which had aroused the indignation of the Earl of Shaftesbury in the House of Lords, also infuriated the young lad working in a pawn-broker's shop in Nottingham. When William Booth was seventeen he began preaching on street corners. But when he led his groups of hearers into church services, ragged and dirty creatures, as a rule, the regular church members did not approve. So William broke away gradually from all connection with sectarian religion.

It must have been a striking spectacle to see this teen-age youth, with his pale face and raven-black hair, preaching on street corners to knots of shabby men and women in the evenings after work hours. And he soon made a reputation for himself as an eloquent speaker. He realized the physical needs of the poor, but he saw also the results in their lives of evil, especially liquor, and he knew from experience that these people who listened to him with deep interest would never be welcomed inside chapels and churches.

To show how William Booth felt the poverty of the people around him, here is an incident that happened while he was still in his early teens and before he began preaching. He and a friend once came upon a poor old beggar woman dressed in rags and saw that she slept in doorways or under hedges. "See here," said William, "something must be done!"

"Agreed!" said his friend, and together they collected a little money, found a small cabin, begged some furniture for it, and turned it over to the poor creature with the promise of money to be paid regularly for fuel and food. This money came mostly out of William's small earnings at the pawn shop.

In time he found his way from the slums of Nottingham to the worst slums of London. In 1855 he married a noble woman, Catherine Mumford, who came to be known as "the Mother of the Salvation Army." She was like his right arm, although she was never in strong health and died many years before her husband. In London, Booth got hold of an old woolen mill that was no longer in operation. This he made over into the headquarters for his "Mission," as he called it then.

It was no easy life he had chosen. Respectable people criticized his preaching as too emotional; and among the crowds that listened on street corners or sat in his mission hall, there were often toughs who came to shout insults at him. The city police didn't like what they called Booth's "parading" and "obstructing traffic." Although he had a powerful will and a fiery temper, he never lost control of a situation. He seemed to have a knack for handling hoodlums, policemen, and, most of all, the respectable rich people who sneered at what he was trying to do.

In 1878 William Booth made an important decision. He made his followers into a military organization with army titles. He thought at first of calling it the "Volunteer Army," but at that time the word volunteer was being laughed at in Britain, because it was only the professional soldier who was supposed to be of any use. So another name was finally adopted, the "Salvation Army," a name the organization has borne ever since.

This meant uniforms for both men and women, and military discipline in both giving and obeying orders. Naturally, William Booth, the founder, was the first General, a rank that he held until his death. Mrs. Booth designed the uniforms for the women, adopting the poke bonnet which she had worn as a girl in the eighteen-forties and fifties.

The work of the Salvation Army grew steadily, against constant opposition and ridicule, especially from the liquor interests. Sometimes a Salvation Army parade would bring on a street riot staged by hired toughs. But the work went on. General Booth knew that his was the only organization reaching a helping hand to the outcast of the city slums; nobody else seemed to care.

In 1890, Booth, with the help of a great journalist, W. T. Stead, wrote a book entitled, *In Darkest England And The Way Out.* This title was an echo of a famous book by the explorer Henry M. Stanley, *In Darkest Africa.* The Booth volume revealed the sufferings of the slum-dwellers, not only in London and Liverpool, but in all the cities of England. It created a sensation. Many readers were so horrified and angry at what the author revealed that they turned on him with fury. Even the great scientist Thomas H. Huxley bitterly denounced William Booth and his book. The truth was not pleasant. But *Darkest England* resulted in a new interest in slum problems on the part of both churchmen and politicians.

In that same year, 1890, Mrs. Booth died, but her husband carried on more than a score of years longer. In his old age, with his long white beard and dignified bearing, he looked, people said, "like an old Hebrew prophet come back to life." He was sought out by leading men and women who now realized the greatness of his crusade for the poor. King Edward VII sent for him once and the two men had a very friendly talk. One day the South African magnate, Cecil Rhodes, found himself in the same railroad coach with General Booth. They quickly became acquainted, and before they parted, the two knelt down together in prayer. On another occasion, the great statesman, William Ewart Gladstone, sent for Booth and they had a long talk over cups of tea on the problems of the poor.

The whole mission of General Booth and his Salvation Army may be summed up in his own memorable words: "The first step in saving outcasts consists in making them feel that some decent human being cares enough for them to take an interest in the question whether they rise or sink." And his own personal career may be expressed in the words he spoke when, as a youth, still in his teens, he had determined on a life of service: "God shall have all there is of William Booth." No resolution was ever more nobly lived up to.

Evangeline Cory Booth, "The White Angel of the Slums"

On Christmas Day, 1865, a girl was born to the Booths, the seventh of a family of eight children. No one could have guessed that this infant was destined to be a rare Christmas gift, not only to her parents and to the Salvation Army, but to the poor and needy, the sick and crippled, the socially outcast and innocent sufferers as well, in Britain and America, or that some day she would be known to a large part of the world by the loving title, "The White Angel of the Slums."

The year in which she was born happened to be the very year in which her parents opened their mission in the London slums. In all her long life she never knew any other existence than service in the Salvation Army. And she, more than anyone else in the family, picked up the flag when it fell from her father's dying hands and carried it on into a world-wide mission that even the old General had never dreamed of. When she finished her life story, the Salvation Army that began as only a handful of devoted men and women in London had nearly fourteen million in uniform, serving ninety-seven countries and territories, and speaking one hundred and two languages.

The little baby born on that Christmas Day in 1865 was named Eva by her parents, and she went by that name until, as she grew up, she decided that she would rather be called Evangeline, which she probably took from Longfellow's famous poem. The Booth children had a strict religious bringing up, but Eva and her brothers didn't mind because their father encouraged them to play games made up out of Bible stories when indoors, and outdoors he loved to hear them romping and shouting with the neighbors' children, even if they were poor and ragged.

From the first the Booth children were taught that they were there in that shabby part of London in order to help those who were in need, and Eva thought it as much fun to run helpful errands as to play games. She was still only a child when she got a woman who was out of work started at a little business in an unoccupied cellar. Eva put out a sign reading, "All broken toys mended here. Dolls manufactured." Then she went from house to house where there were children, begging legs, arms and heads of broken dolls. Next she went to a carpenter's shop and begged bags of sawdust. Soon the woman was doing a flourishing business.

Meanwhile Eva's parents discovered that she had a sweet and strong singing voice. Often, in his indoor meetings, William Booth would announce, "My little Eva will now sing for us." With not a trace of stage fright, the child would stand up on the platform and lead off in a familiar hymn. To her this was fun, too.

As she grew into her early teens, she learned to play the accordion; with a shawl over her head she would go to the busy areas of the city, such as Piccadilly Circus and, standing on the steps of a building, sing and play, with a cup ready for pennies or shillings. She let people know that the money was for the poor to buy coal, and with her beauty and sweet voice she did well. Once she dressed herself like a flower girl, in shabby frock and darned stockings, again to make money for her father's mission, and the story is that she did fully as well in sales as the professional flower girls.

As she grew to a beautiful young womanhood, she had a romance. She had many suitors, but her preference was a young Russian prince. He was a sincere Christian, too, but Evangeline—by this time she was not Eva any longer—realized that he could not possibly fit into the Salvation Army. And so, with a deep pang, she gave him up because she felt that she must give her whole life to the Cause. And she never married.

For a while she held the office in London of Field Commissioner. Then for nine years she was in Canada as Commander of the Salvation Army there. In 1898 she organized and equipped a party for relief work among the miners in the Alaska gold rush of that year. Six years later she was appointed Commander-in-Chief in the United States. Here, in this country, she gave her life for the next thirty years. That period was briefly interrupted only by her return to London during World War I.

Although she was in London supervising all the war work of the Salvation Army, she had a special interest in what the Salvationists could do for the American doughboys in France after we entered the war. "You must go," she said, "wherever the American soldiers are ordered to go." She consulted General Pershing, who agreed to accept the help of the Salvation Army and gave the men and women a special epaulette to wear to identify them among the troops in many other uniforms. These Salvationists followed the armies well up to the front lines, serving hot coffee and doughnuts to the soldiers as they went slogging along the muddy roads of France to their trenches. The doughboys would sing out, "Hi, Sal!" whenever they saw a lassie with her canteen, Sal being short for Salvation Army. And it soon became Sally.

It was a service full of hardships, but so well performed that these devoted people endeared themselves to the American soldiers, even to those who would never have listened to their preaching at home. One old officer of the regular army wrote, "I wish every American who stood on street corners and sneered at the work of the Salvation Army could see what they are doing for the boys in France."

The inspiration for all this service was Evangeline Booth. In later years the work has greatly broadened. The Salvation Army maintains rescue homes, shelters, boarding houses for women, industrial homes and shelters for men, day nurseries for children, settlements in slum areas, fresh air camps, missing persons bureaus, legal advice for the poor, and even at that the list is not nearly complete.

In 1934 Evangeline Booth was elected General, with headquarters in London, but five years later she resigned that top rank and returned to continue leading the work in America. Meanwhile, honors were fairly showered on her, from gold medals to honorary degrees from universities, all for her services to humanity.

It might be added that Evangeline was the author and composer of many of the Salvation Army hymns that are still sung, and she wrote numerous articles and books about the work of her organization.

In 1950 this saintly woman came to the end of her life in Hartsdale, a suburb of New York. But the work begun by her parents in the service of humanity goes on all over the world. We may think of William Booth and his daughter Evangeline as soldiers of a new kind of army, one that aims not to wound or kill, but to heal and to save. Not long ago, in war-torn Germany, a Salvation Army General, Albert Osborn, was introduced to an audience by the Lord Mayor of Cologne, who said, "I am not a military man but I love this Army!"

To this the General replied, "We have a uniform and we have a flag. But that flag has never caused strife. We seek to bring all nations together in peace."

Evangeline Booth was a great soldier in this army, a worthy daughter of its founder. People who knew her often said, "This is one of the world's great women."

JOSEPH DAMIEN DE VEUSTER
"FATHER DAMIEN"
IRA DUTTON, "BROTHER JOSEPH"

FATHER DAMIEN

IRA DUTTON

X. JOSEPH DAMIEN DE VEUSTER, "FATHER DAMIEN"

January 3, 1840—April 15, 1889

IRA DUTTON, "BROTHER JOSEPH"

April 27, 1843—March 26, 1931

THIS IS THE story of two devoted men and their mission to men, women and children smitten with one of the most dreaded diseases known, leprosy. It is also the most ancient of recorded diseases. We know that it wrought havoc in Egypt as long ago as 3000 B.C. From there it spread to Asia, especially India, and to other parts of Africa. We read about it in the Bible, in both the Old Testament and the New. It appeared in Greece, and Roman armies serving in Egypt brought it to Italy, then to Spain, and later to the German tribes with whom they waged war.

Though it had been common early in medieval times, its spread was greatly increased by the Crusades, which carried it into every corner of Europe, counting its victims from king to serf. But it was England that suffered most. In the twelfth century, one-third of that nation's population of two and a half million were lepers. But, strange to say, the Black Death, a plague that wiped out thousands of towns and villages in Europe, seemed to have a somewhat similar effect on leprosy, because after that pestilence leprosy began to disappear. By the sixteenth century it had practically vanished in Europe, though it was still rampant in Asia.

Famous Humanitarians

In medieval Europe there were severe rules for the lepers. It was believed that this disease was a punishment for sin. But, in spite of this cruel notion, there was a kindly care practiced by the monasteries, so that a leper in Europe was more gently treated than a leper elsewhere in the world.

This disease was not known in America before the Europeans came, and it has always been rare in this hemisphere. But when the Yankee whalers and clipper ships touched at the Hawaiian Islands on their way to and from China ports, they brought leprosy from China to these islands with dreadful results. Before 1860 it had become a plague among the natives. In that year one of the islands was selected as the site of a leper colony, in order to segregate the diseased persons from those whom they might contaminate. This island was Molokai, a beautiful area thirty-seven miles long and ten miles wide, lying about twenty-five miles east of Honolulu. It has a mountain range running the length of the island, and on the north shore the map shows a small projection jutting out like a thorn. The rest of the island has pineapple plantations and cattle ranches, but it is this little spur on the north shore that has made the name Molokai known the world over, for this is the spot that was selected for the leper colony.

The reason for choosing this piece of land was that it was bounded by the ocean on two sides and on the land side by a cliff sixteen hundred feet high, which even able-bodied men would not care to climb. These physical features would deter any leper from escaping.

At first the inmates of the colony were merely taken there and left, with only occasional supplies of food. During the early years, both Catholic and Protestant missionaries went there for brief visits. Some caught the disease and died there; others, deciding that the work was hopeless, came away.

In the early sixties and seventies, there was a young Belgian priest in Hawaii who heard from his bishop of the dreadful conditions of the leper colony. This priest was Joseph Damien de Veuster, known as Father Damien. Born and educated in Belgium, he had entered a religious order and in 1863 had been sent out as a missionary to Hawaii. It was ten years later that he listened to his bishop addressing a gathering of priests, describing the leper colony at Molokai, saying with what deep regret he had to admit that it was impossible to accomplish anything for the poor creatures there. The word impossible struck fire in the heart of the young priest. Was anything impossible in the service of God? The very hopelessness of the picture appealed to him, and he begged the Bishop to let him go and work for those unhappy creatures, to relieve their physical misery and to give them spiritual hope.

Some of the lepers had sent a request to the Bishop for a resident priest, but he had been unwilling to condemn anyone to such a duty. Here, however, was an eager volunteer. The answer was a "Yes, and God be with you." At that moment there was a ship in the harbor ready to sail for Molokai with fifty lepers aboard. Within two hours of his getting permission from the Bishop, the young priest was on board. He did not even wait to say good-bye to his friends or to pack supplies and extra clothing.

When he arrived, his eyes fell upon a dreadful scene. He found that the victims of this hopeless and loathsome disease were existing in two villages consisting of grass huts that let in wind and rain. The air was full of horrible stenches, for there was no sanitation. The lepers themselves were filthy. The water supply was too precious to use for washing, and at that was hardly fit to drink. There was no one to care for the ones who were dying.

As for himself, Father Damien had to sleep on the bare ground for many weeks after he landed. His only shelter was a tree, and in his rest he was tortured by swarms of insects. At first his idea was that he might stay with the lepers for a period of two or three weeks to see what he could do, but when that time was past he wrote to the Bishop asking that he might be allowed to stay on indefinitely. Again the answer was yes. And so began a life career in ministering to lepers, one so devoted and so unsparing of himself that this obscure young priest became renowned and admired all over the civilized world.

He found that a little Catholic chapel had already been built before his arrival, but he took on many more duties than those of a priest. He taught the children, he did such medical work as he knew how, he built houses with his own hands, made coffins and dug the graves. For when he arrived he discovered that eighty per cent of the inmates were desperately ill, and that there was death in every hut.

Famous Humanitarians

The conditions of living at Molokai were so horrible that he made a report to the Board of Health created by the Hawaiian king. After some weeks he returned to Honolulu to get supplies that were desperately needed and to try to interest the authorities. But the President of the Board of Health refused. He called Father Damien headstrong, and ordered him back to Molokai, never to leave again. If he once showed himself in Honolulu, he would face arrest!

Fortunately, after six months there was a new king and a new President of the Board of Health, who countermanded that senseless order. Yet Father Damien found that he always had to battle with the Board for every little benefit he tried to get for his lepers.

In his great work during the years that followed, Father Damien was helped by several priests for short periods, and in 1889 by three Franciscan Sisters who arrived to take care of orphan girls. In time, an orphanage was started for orphan boys, too, and regular schools were organized. Father Damien managed to work near miracles. But one Sunday morning in 1885 the congregation in his church—which he had built with his own hands—was startled to hear him begin his sermon, not with the customary Brethren, but with the new phrase, "We lepers." According to his close friend and helper, Ira Dutton, the "Brother Joseph" who came to work by his side the next year, the priest had suspected as early as 1884 that he had contracted leprosy. He told Dutton that one morning while shaving he had upset a mug of scalding water on his bare foot, but had felt nothing. This made him suspect that he had contracted leprosy, and in a few months that suspicion proved all too true. In his case the infection settled chiefly in his lungs.

The news shocked the world. The Bishop begged Father Damien to go to Honolulu for treatment, but in those days there was no remedy.

"Why don't you rest?" the priest was asked.

"Rest? It's no time to rest now, when there is so much left to do and my time is so short." And again he said, "I would not be cured if the price of my cure were that I must leave the Island and give up my work."

It was not strange that he became a victim of leprosy because he was so thoughtless of self that he did not take necessary precautions. He handled the same tools that the lepers did, a leper cooked his food and another washed his clothes. Sometimes a leper would come in and lie down on the priest's bed! There were a hundred ways in which he could have caught the infection. However, he was able to go about his duties until March, 1889, when he finally had to give up. On the fifteenth of the following April, the earthly career of this shining spirit came to an end.

The news of his death brought tributes of praise from all over the world, and liberal gifts not only for the betterment of the Molokai colony, but for better treatment of lepers everywhere.

Ira Dutton, "Brother Joseph"

Mention has already been made above of a man named Dutton who came to the Molokai colony as a volunteer helper to Father Damien. He became the intimate friend of the priest during the years when the latter was slowly breaking under the disease, and he took over the mission on Father Damien's death. Ira Dutton was an American, born on a farm in the village of Stowe, Vermont. When he was four, his father moved to Wisconsin and there the boy grew up. When the Civil War came, he volunteered and served four years in the Army of the Cumberland. He enjoyed an unusual army career, for in all that time he was never wounded and never sick for a single day!

After the war Dutton accepted a government job, which he held until 1883. For a while in this period he fell a victim to drink, then he pulled himself together and broke the habit. Ever after he had the feeling of having wasted his life, and he wanted to make up for it if he could. Naturally, he turned to religion, and eventually he became a Catholic. He spent twenty months in a monastery, but never became a monk or member of any religious order.

One day, while reading in a convent library in St. Louis, he came upon the story of Father Damien at Molokai. Here was just the sort of completely self-sacrificing work for the unfortunate that he wanted to do. At once he settled his affairs and then made the long trip to San Francisco by sailing vessel. From San Francisco he took passage to Honolulu.

Famous Humanitarians

Before being permitted to go to Molokai, Ira Dutton had to obtain the permission of the Board of Health. He was helped in his application by the fact that he had been trained during the war in the treatment of sores and wounds. It all took time, but finally, in July, 1886, Dutton landed on the beach at Molokai. As he was welcomed by Father Damien, the newcomer could see in the face of the priest the ravages of the fatal disease. From the moment that they grasped hands, the two men became fast friends. Although Ira Dutton was not a member of any Catholic order, he asked to be called, not Ira Dutton, but "Brother Joseph," after Saint Joseph, his patron saint. Having no monk's or priest's robe, he made a sort of uniform for himself, consisting of a suit of simple blue denim. This was for him his religious costume, and he never wore anything else during the many years that he worked for the lepers at Molokai.

It was no easy life that he had chosen for himself. He got up at four-thirty every morning, and all day long he would go from hut to hut, cleaning and dressing the lepers' sores. He was busy at this work until late at night. In this treatment he always followed the best medical advice. He was orderly and systematic, and at the same time he was careful to guard against infection, washing his hands often. Although all who knew about him predicted that his close contact with the lepers would surely give him the disease, this did not come true, although he worked among them for forty-five years.

It was a great comfort to the dying priest to know that his own mission would be continued by Brother Joseph so efficiently and devotedly. "I die now," said he, "knowing that Brother Joseph will care for my orphans." Before the end he asked his friend to enter the priesthood, but Brother Joseph's answer was a simple "I am not fit."

After Father Damien's death, important changes took place. When Hawaii became a territory of the United States, conditions at the leper colony quickly took a turn for the better. And in 1910, a new treatment for leprosy came out of India, the use of Chaulmoogra oil. Medical science improved the treatment until, for the first time in the history of the world, some lepers were actually cured by medicine. Today, Molokai is not the horrible, hopeless place for those dying of a loathsome disease as it was when Father Damien first landed there, and was still, even at the time Ira Dutton arrived. It is a modern leprosarium, or hospital, with all the benefits of modern medicine to effect cures, for nowadays few cases are considered hopeless.

One event at Molokai must be mentioned that took place many years after Father Damien's death. In December, 1907, President Theodore Roosevelt sent our battle fleet on a journey round the world. The gray-bearded old veteran on Molokai heard about that cruise, and he wrote to the President asking that the fleet be ordered on its Pacific route to steam near enough to this island for the lepers to see it, for that would be a thrilling event in their dull lives. The President had known about Ira Dutton's work and was happy to grant his request. He went further by ordering that each of the sixteen ships, as it paraded past in single file, should salute the old soldier who would be standing on the shore watching.

Word was sent to Dutton as to just when to expect to see the fleet, and he and his leper "boys" stood beside the flagstaff near the beach. It was the proudest day of Dutton's life. Overhead flew the Stars and Stripes. He stood bareheaded, with his precious binoculars—his dearest possession—in his hand, watching for the first streak of smoke on the horizon. Right on time, the leader of the great, gray battleships forged into view. In perfect formation the others followed, and each, as it passed the point of land on which the leper colony stood, dipped her flag in salute. Perhaps no king ever received such an impressive honor as this elderly man in shabby blue denim, with his tousled gray hair and beard, standing at attention there on the beach, with tears of pride running down his cheeks. And all around in the background stood the members of the leper colony, eager and thrilled. After the parade was over, Dutton wrote a letter to the President thanking him, and in reply he received a photograph of Theodore Roosevelt, signed, "To Brother Joseph, with all good wishes."

When World War I broke out in 1917, Dutton wrote to another President, Woodrow Wilson, offering to organize a few hundred Civil War veterans into a sharpshooter outfit, to be dressed in their old blue uniforms, as an inspiration to the young men at home. This request was denied as impracticable, but the old patriot kept busy with Red Cross work and Liberty Bond drives as far as he could. He lent his fine binoculars to the Government for the duration of the war; they were used by the Navy and returned to him with thanks after the Armistice.

Another Chief Executive took notice of this man's noble devotion to the lepers. President Harding wrote Ira Dutton a long letter of appreciation and admiration.

Until 1920 Brother Joseph enjoyed fine health, but in that year he fell victim to the influenza epidemic that swept the world after the war. "I was really ill," he confessed, "for the first time in my life." Indeed, he was never the same afterward. Eight years later, he had a breakdown, but still he kept busy and would not permit anyone else to raise or lower the flag, morning and evening. By this time he was eighty-five years old, and his eyes and hearing were failing him badly. More illness followed, and then he was taken to Honolulu for an operation to restore his sight.

In February, 1931, the Territorial Government voted him $300 a month, a rather late recognition of his service at the leper colony without pay. A few weeks later, on March 26, he died. On his coffin was spread the flag he had served both in war and in peace during a long life. No better epitaph can be chosen for him than the reply he made to a question why, as a layman, he called himself Brother Joseph.

"That," said he, "is because I want to be a brother to everybody."

JACOB AUGUST RIIS
JANE ADDAMS

JACOB RIIS

JANE ADDAMS

XI. JACOB AUGUST RIIS

May 3, 1849—May 26, 1914

JANE ADDAMS

September 6, 1860—May 21, 1935

J ACOB RIIS was one of those foreign-born citizens who became distinguished Americans. Born in the ancient town of Ribe in Denmark, the son of a teacher in the local Latin school, Jacob received most of his education from his father. From him, too, he learned something of journalism, because the father edited a weekly paper, and he taught his son how copy should be prepared for the press and how it should be read in proof. This training proved valuable in later years when the young man was looking for work in an American newspaper office.

The elder Riis hoped that his boy would become a professor of Latin, following in the paternal footsteps. But Jacob wasn't interested in Latin. In fact, the only language subject that appealed to him was English, because Charles Dickens's magazine, *All the Year Round*, came regularly into the Riis home and Jacob wanted to be able to read the stories. Since the lad disliked school, his father stopped his formal education when the boy was fourteen and apprenticed him to a carpenter in Copenhagen.

Just before he became a carpenter's apprentice, an incident happened which foreshadowed his future mission in life. When he was only thirteen years old, he discovered a very old, tumble-down tenement known as Rag

Hall. It had been built over an open drain and this was choked with rats' nests. The animals themselves scuttled through every part of the building. Of course, plenty of grown-ups knew about the condition in Rag Hall—which might well have been called Rat Hall, but it took this boy, Jacob Riis, to do something about it.

At Christmas he had been given a silver coin, and he still had it. He took it to the head of the poorest family in the tenement, asking him to use it for cleaning up the place. The man agreed, though he must have been astonished at such a request from a boy, and put it into a job of whitewashing. Jacob himself concentrated on cleaning out the rats' nests in the drains and killing the rats. He did a thorough job.

What this lad of thirteen did to Rag Hall he was destined to do over and over again on a huge scale for a great city thousands of miles away, New York. When he was eighteen, he had finished his apprenticeship to the carpenter; but when he went back to Ribe to see his sweetheart, he discovered that her parents frowned on him because he was only a common carpenter. At that he decided that he would do something else for a career, and suggested to his parents that he might go to America and make his fortune. They consented. The neighbors, who must have been fond of the youth, made up a purse of forty dollars to help him on the long journey. Finally, in the year 1870, when he was twenty-one, he landed in New York.

For a long time, however, America seemed anything but a land of opportunity to Jacob Riis. He tried anything and everything that would keep him alive. He left the city, worked on a farm, tried bricklaying, coal-mining in Pennsylvania, and some carpentering here and there, but not for long. "I was tired of hammer and saw," he wrote afterward. He finally returned to New York and arrived there with exactly one cent in his pocket.

What followed for a while was a tough life, especially for a young man brought up in a comfortable, cultured home. He found himself forced sometimes to sleep in doorways or in dreadful places called police lodging houses, filled with the riffraff of the slums. It was a school of hard knocks for Jacob Riis, but he learned by this experience what people herded in our city slums

Jacob August Riis

have to face in trying to keep alive. However, it did not make him sour. In his later years he wrote these words about what that hard life taught him:

"As to battling with the world, that is good for a young man, much better than to hang on to somebody for support. When you have fought your way through a tight place you are better for it. I am afraid this is not the case when you are shoved through."

Certainly, no one seems to have given this young immigrant any friendly shove!

Finally, he turned to newspaper work and in 1877 managed to land a job on a famous newspaper, the New York *Tribune*, as a police reporter. Here he made good, and stayed with that paper for the next eleven years. After that he went to another famous paper, the New York *Sun*, and wrote for it during another eleven years.

It was this work as a police reporter, backed by his own experience as a penniless immigrant, which led him to his life work, reforming the slums of New York. For, to get the facts of a story which he would hear about at police headquarters, he would go to the actual scene, and this took him through many a foul tenement of the Lower East Side. More than once he must have been reminded of that rat-infested tenement in his native town, which he cleaned up as a boy.

Evidently he had made a good start in mastering English before he left for America and picked up the tricks of speech quickly after arriving here, because no one who reads any one of his many books would suspect from the style that it was written by a foreigner. Before he began writing books, his pictures in the newspapers of the conditions in the slum districts were so vivid that they attracted wide attention. Soon he was in great demand as a lecturer, and then followed the first of his books, *How the Other Half Lives* (1890). This made a sensation, revealing as it did, shocking conditions of filth, disease, vice, and crime in the parts of New York where immigrants were crowded together like animals. This book went into many editions.

One of Jacob Riis's most spectacular achievements had to do not with the slum and the foreigner, but something that came into the home of the rich as well as the poor. Looking one day at the weekly analysis of the water coming into the city from the Croton River, he noticed the phrase, "just a trace of nitrates." At once he suspected pollution, and singlehanded, armed with a camera, he spent a week tracing every stream that ran into the Croton River. He discovered what he had suspected from the first, that the city water supply was contaminated with sewage. His articles in the paper, illustrated with photographs, created such a sensation that the Board of Health took over the situation and soon the city bought the entire Croton River watershed, in order to keep the water clean.

That was only one of his victories. He was specially interested in the conditions surrounding the life of the children of the slums, and he wrote books about them. He found that the public schools were dark and badly overcrowded, with only basements for playgrounds for over a thousand children. In all Manhattan he discovered only one outdoor playground attached to a public school, and that was an old graveyard!

This story, too, aroused the good people of New York, and as a result the entire public school system was reformed. Sixty new school buildings were put up, a Playground Association was formed, and some of the vilest spots on the East Side were cleared of their filthy tenements and transformed into little parks.

There was another evil affecting the children which Jacob Riis exposed and fought. This was the fact that, contrary to law, but with false age certificates furnished too often by the parents, children under fourteen were made to work long hours in factories. He found a way to put a stop to that.

Perhaps he took the greatest pride in what he was able to do for a section of the slums called Mulberry Bend, known as the worst tenement block for overcrowding, vice, disease, and crime in all New York. When he finished with it, there was a Mulberry Bend Park and a Neighborhood House, later named after him.

Meanwhile, it might be told that Jacob Riis in time married the sweetheart of his boyhood days, the very one whose parents told him that they were not going to let their daughter marry a common carpenter, and brought her back to America. The Riis family made their home in the suburbs of New York,

Jacob August Riis

and the five children born to them were so impressed with their father's description of the slum children who never had a glimpse of green grass, flowers and trees, that they used to gather armfuls of daisies in the fields and give them to their father to take to "the poors," as they called these underprivileged children. The father always distributed them to the children in the slums, most of whom hardly knew what a flower was.

Naturally, in all this crusading, Jacob Riis made powerful enemies. The owners of the tenements, the politicians who worked hand in hand with the crooks, all did their best to block his reforms. Indeed, it is a wonder that he did not suffer death or injury at the hands of the mobsters. But, somehow, he was too much for them all. His pen was his battle lance, and with that he won all the way.

It should be added, too, that such a man as Jacob Riis made powerful friends, too. Chief of these was Theodore Roosevelt. First as Police Commissioner of New York, then as Governor of the State, and finally as President of the United States, Roosevelt let it be known that he had the greatest admiration for Jacob Riis. He offered him high official posts, but Riis always declined. "I'm too busy," he explained, "to enter politics." And this is what Theodore Roosevelt wrote about him in later years. "Jacob Riis was the most useful American of his day. He came the nearest to the ideal of an American citizen . . . a brother to all men, especially the unfortunate." And that was no mean tribute coming from another great American.

How Jacob Riis came to realize suddenly that he was not just a transplanted Dane, but a genuine American, is told on the last page of his autobiography, *The Making of an American*. It happened while he was in Denmark on a visit to see his mother. He fell sick in Elsinore and was in bed for weeks. When the fever left him, he still felt sick and discouraged. But from a window he could glimpse the sea even as he lay on the pillow.

"All at once there sailed past, close inshore, a ship flying the flag of freedom blown out on the breeze till every star in it shone bright and clear. That moment I knew. Gone were illness, discouragement and gloom! Forgotten weakness and suffering, the cautions of doctor and nurse. I sat up in bed and shouted, laughed and cried by turns, waving my handkerchief to the flag out there. They thought that I had lost my head, but I told them no, thank God! I had found it, and my heart too, at last. I knew then it was my flag, that my children's home was mine, indeed; that I also had become an American in truth. And I thanked God, and like the man sick of the palsy, arose from my bed and went home healed."

In 1904 Riis was suddenly stricken with heart disease, and thereafter he had to be careful. He knew he could not keep up his exhausting program of writing, lecturing and leading reform movements. He always hated being called a reformer, because the word sounded too smug and self-righteous. He had what not all reformers possess, a sense of humor, humility, and a tender heart. His personality as well as his facts helped him win victories. The end came in 1914 at his country home in Barre, Massachusetts. Since he hated the word reformer as applied to himself, we shall leave him with a phrase that one of his admirers used to describe him, "Jacob Riis, the Great Emancipator of the Slums."

Jane Addams

Of course, New York was not the only great city in America with foul areas, nor was Jacob Riis the only crusader who battled against the evils of city slums. Another who deserves to stand beside Jacob Riis is the subject of the rest of this chapter, Jane Addams.

Jane was neither an immigrant child nor was she born poor. Her father was a prosperous mill owner of Cedarville, Illinois, and he was liked and admired by a large circle of friends. Among these friends was Abraham Lincoln. In fact, one of Jane's earliest memories was of seeing, as a child of five, all the houses of the town draped in black at the news of Lincoln's assassination.

About two years later, she went one day with her father on one of his visits to the mill district and she noticed the sort of houses in which the mill workers lived. "Why do these people live in such horrid little houses, Papa?"

"Because they are poor."

"Well," the seven-year-old girl announced, "when I get to be big, I'm going to have a big house, but it isn't going to be between other big houses, it's going to be between horrid little houses like these."

It was a strangely prophetic thing for the child to say, for after she grew up that was exactly what she did. Her famous Hull House was a big old-fashioned mansion which she transformed into a neighborhood center of good will in the very heart of the Chicago slums.

As a child, Jane was troubled by a slight curvature of the spine. In her young womanhood she began the study of medicine as the best road to relieve suffering, but her affliction came back so severely as to lay her in bed. Then the doctors told her that she must give up her medical studies and take two years of rest in Europe. While in London, riding on the top of a bus, she had a horrifying glimpse of what a big city slum is like. Then and there she decided to devote her life to doing good to slum-dwellers, and there was no better place to begin than Chicago, which was not far from her home town.

In those days it is said that of Chicago's million inhabitants, 750,000 were foreign-born. And these people—Italians, Bohemians, Germans, Polish and Russian Jews, French Canadians, and Irish—each occupied its own section of the city, and unfortunately they brought over from the Old World the age-old hatreds and suspicions between nations, religions and races. Miss Addams discovered that the whole slum area was composed of rotten tenements, stables, outhouses and saloons. There was plenty that needed to be done.

It was in January, 1889, that this young woman, not yet thirty, and her friend, Ellen Starr, took over a big house which had been built in 1856 by a pioneer citizen named Hull. At the time these young women arrived, the house was badly run down and surrounded by slums. It was Jane Addams's idea to transform this old house into a welfare center for the people who lived around it.

At first these people were suspicious. Why should a rich young woman set up a place like this unless she was trying to get something out of them? Her answer was to refurnish the old mansion, make it a place from which went out deeds of kindness, and before long the scowls gave way to smiles.

It was not only a hard but a brave thing for a girl in her twenties to take on herself, for the slums reeked with crime as well as filth, but her motto in life was, "Always do what you are afraid to do." How the criminals were arm-in-arm with the politicians and the police is suggested by the fact that the drug stores around Hull House in those days sold cocaine, even to schoolchildren, openly, despite the law. And, like Jacob Riis in New York, Jane Addams had the tenement landlord, the crooked politician, and the gangster against her all the way.

It is a long and shining story of what Miss Addams did with her "big house between horrid little houses." For forty years she worked there, and all that time she was active in all other movements that she believed to be good. In 1915, for example, she was elected President of the International Congress of Women at the Hague in Holland, and as head of one of two delegations, she went from one warring country to another, striving to end World War I by negotiations. Mr. Herbert Hoover obtained her help in working for the women and children who were victims of the war, especially in Belgium. In 1931 she was awarded the Nobel Peace Prize, which she shared with Dr. Butler, President of Columbia University. On the occasion of presenting the award, the Norwegian Chairman addressed her as "America's Uncrowned Queen."

Four years later, she died suddenly. At once tributes poured in from all over the civilized world. One European wrote of her as "the one saint that America has produced." In her lifetime she wrote many books and articles, and was often called on to lecture on her work, but, as someone said, "Her masterpiece is her life."

A public funeral was held at Hull House in order that the humble people for whom she had devoted her life might pay her their last tribute of gratitude and love. For two days her body lay in state as if she had been a real queen, and during that time about fifty thousand people filed past. Many of them knelt a moment and offered a prayer, many more had tears streaming down their faces. For they all knew that in her they had lost their best friend.

Here, indeed, was a rare humanitarian, a woman born to wealth and comfort, hampered by ill-health, but who devoted her life to help the outcast and miserable in the squalid streets of Chicago's slums, seeking no reward but the joy of seeing good overcome evil, hope and joy taking the place of despair.

SIR WILFRED THOMASON GRENFELL

SIR WILFRED GRENFELL

XII. SIR WILFRED THOMASON GRENFELL

February 28, 1865—October 9, 1940

ONE OF THE MOST stirring poems in the English language is Tennyson's "Ballad of the Revenge," which tells of an English admiral, Sir Richard Grenville, who, rather than run away from a Spanish fleet, deliberately sailed his ship, the *Revenge*, through the midst of fifty-three enemy vessels, with his guns blazing, until he was overwhelmed by superior numbers. The hero of this sketch was a descendant of that sixteenth-century sea dog. It is true that Sir Wilfred spelled his name differently from Sir Richard, but as he himself remarked, his doughty ancestor spelled his own name in three different ways in one letter. In the sixteenth century a gentleman enjoyed the privilege of spelling as he saw fit. At any rate, the old admiral would have been proud of his descendant, even though Sir Wilfred won his knighthood, not by courage in battle, but by courage in the service of his neglected and sick countrymen living in a bleak land.

Wilfred was born in a pleasant home near Cheshire, England. His father was headmaster of a school, and his mother, born in India, was the daughter of a colonel. The Grenfell home was near the mouth of the River Dee, and the sands of Dee were the boy's favorite playground. When he entered his teens, he was sent to a famous boys' school, Marlborough, attended chiefly by the sons and grandsons of army officers.

When it came to choosing a career, however, he decided against the army and set his heart on medicine. He took one term at Oxford, and then plunged into medical studies at London University, at that time the medical school attached to the great London Hospital, the largest in Britain. Although he did himself credit in his studies, Wilfred was no bookworm. In fact, he was physically what every red-blooded boy would wish to be, for he was a born athlete. Not only did he have a superb physique, but he was gifted with that knack of being a star at every sport that he tried. He rowed, he played Rugby football and cricket, he boxed, he threw the hammer. In each sport he made a name for himself. If in those student years anyone had told him that he would some day be one of the world's great humanitarians, he would have roared with laughter.

One night, however, as he was returning to his quarters after a visit to one of the hospital's out-patients, he had to pass through the outskirts of the slum section near the London Hospital. There he came upon a large tent in an open lot and heard singing going on inside. "Wonder what's happening here," he said to himself and went in. He found there a congregation assembled to listen to a famous pair of American evangelists, Dwight L. Moody and Ira D. Sankey. Wilfred sat down to watch what was going on. Soon a man got up and began a long-winded oration to God that he thought was a prayer. After it had gone on too long, Mr. Moody arose and said, "While our brother finishes his prayer, let's sing a hymn." The congregation burst into a familiar hymn, and "our brother" got quickly to his amen.

This practical way of handling a bore so tickled the young man that he decided to stay and see the meeting through. After Mr. Moody rose to speak, Wilfred found himself interested, and then more deeply moved than he had ever been before. He had always been a fine, upright lad, but religion hadn't meant much to him. He had put all his thought into his medical studies and his spare time into athletics. Now something new had entered his life. As the evangelist described the self-sacrificing life of Jesus, always in behalf of others, a new resolve was born in the young man's heart to make his own life one of service to humanity.

This incident took place in 1885. The following year he passed his examinations as a member of the College of Physicians and the Royal College of Surgeons.

Faithful to his high resolve, he chose for his first practice the roughest field of medicine England had to offer a young doctor; namely, the fishermen of

Sir Wilfred Thomason Grenfell

the North Sea. There was a small group of men interested in bettering the life of these fishermen. They had chartered a small fishing smack and used to go among the vessels of the fishing fleet to hold religious services and to carry first aid. These men needed a doctor, for the fishermen were gone for weeks at a time, and there was much sickness and many accidents aboard their little vessels. Unfortunately, there was a rival group also interested in these fishermen, the London liquor interests. During slack seasons they would send out a "grog boat" to sell the men rum, with evil effects on the men and their families back home.

When young Dr. Grenfell arrived at the wharf and saw the tiny smack on which he had volunteered to serve, he was so taken aback by its small size that he hesitated. What a wretched little tub! But a voice sang out from its deck a loud and cheery "Welcome! Welcome!" and he stepped aboard. On that day he began his active service for the fishermen, and he made his start in the worst time of year for hardships at sea; namely, midwinter.

It proved to be a tougher job than he had dreamed. He discovered that drink was the worst evil among the fishermen, but he soon found also that he had his hands full tending sick men and mending broken bones. One great result of his mission was the final banishment of the grog ships by means of an international agreement. In addition to his medical work, Grenfell, who was a born sailor, prepared for his examinations as a master mariner, and his knowledge of seamanship was of the greatest help to him in all his later career on the coast of Labrador.

In 1891, Lord Southborough, returning from a trip to Canada and Newfoundland, made a report on the desperate needs of the British fishermen on that coast. As a result, an expedition was fitted out to go to their help. Hearing about this, Dr. Grenfell immediately volunteered to go in one of the small sailing vessels as a doctor. In the spring of 1892 the boats were ready, and he found himself assigned to a tiny ketch, with a freeboard of only three feet above the water line. He had never before crossed the Atlantic, and this vessel was so small that it would make the *Santa Maria* of Columbus look like the *Queen Elizabeth*. But it got across safely and arrived at St. Johns, Newfoundland. It was still bitterly cold, for the chill of near-by icebergs made the April air wintry. For contrast, just as the party arrived, they found the town of St. Johns ablaze, the flames spreading even to some of the vessels at the wharves. Something had gone wrong with the water system so that the firemen were helpless. It was the most unpleasant welcome the mission ketch could have received. But word got ashore that there was a real doctor on board, and despite the fire there came a rush of visitors. A miserable boat slid alongside with a half-dressed man as its oarsman. He hailed Dr. Grenfell. "Be you a real doctor?"

"That's what I call myself."

"Us hasn't got no money, but there's a very sick man ashore, if you'd come and see him."

No second invitation was needed. Grenfell went ashore at once. The man led him to a pitiable hovel made of sods. It had one room, and one window with bits of glass stuck together. The floor consisted of pebbles. A small stove thrust its pipe through a hole in the roof. The earthen walls were oozing moisture. In this dreadful cabin were huddled six children. A swineherd, in the England of Robin Hood, lived in a better home than this sod hovel of a British fisherman at the close of the nineteenth century.

In one corner of that room was a rough bunk in which lay a man coughing hard, while his wife gave him water from a teaspoon. It didn't take the doctor long to realize that the man was near death from pneumonia; that nothing could save him but expert nursing in a hospital, and there was no hospital. Death did come not long after.

That scene Dr. Grenfell found was typical of the entire Labrador and New-foundland coast. Everywhere he went on that year's mission he found disease, injuries, deformities; and desperate hardships for those who were well. One of these was the miserable food. Many families lived the year through on nothing but fish and water. Milk for babies and young children was unheard of. It was just fish and water to keep alive.

On his return to London, Wilfred Grenfell made a report on the conditions, and the following spring he went back with two young doctors and two trained nurses. Soon after his arrival he chose two islands, about two hundred miles apart, as sites for cottage hospitals. Generous gifts began to pour in from the fishery firms and from individuals. Up to the time Grenfell's report was published, no one in Canada, Britain or America had any idea of the misery of these fisherfolk and their desperate need of medical care. And during the seasons when navigation was closed, the doctor made it his business to publish articles and give lectures to publicize the situation.

It is a long and inspiring story of what this man did singlehanded to bring medicines and food and clothing to the coast settlements and to perform operations under the most difficult conditions. It was well that he was a master mariner, for he had to cruise along that treacherous coast, often through rough seas, and make landings through heavy surf. Once the trip was made in a small, wood-burning steam launch. On the way back, the going was so hard that all the fuel was gone, and he barely made home port by breaking up the roof of the cabin and throwing the wood on the fire.

Perhaps his most desperate adventure happened on Easter Sunday, April 21, 1908, when word was brought to him that a man with an infected wound following an operation would die unless he could have an amputation. It was April on the calendar, but the landscape and harbor were still white with snow and ice. The only way to reach the patient was by dog sledge.

Off the doctor went at once, for there was no time to lose. He had eight dogs to drive. At one place he saw what looked like a good ice bridge across a bay, which would be a short cut on the long journey. He knew the ice might be rotten, but to save a life he must take the chance. Off he dashed with his sledge on the ice, but it turned out to be slushy, and soon the whole ice field broke from the shore and started out to sea on the tide. To keep from falling through the rotten ice, Dr. Grenfell flung himself full length, shouting to his dogs to dash back to shore. But after about twenty yards the sledge sank through the slush. Then he cut the dogs loose to save them. Finally, they scrambled together on a floe of frozen snow which held them up, but all the while the ice was drifting out to sea.

Drenched in ice water and exposed to a cutting wind, Dr. Grenfell knew that unless he did something he would soon freeze to death. Reluctantly he killed three of his dogs and wrapped their furry hides around his body. Even at that he felt sure that he must die. But after a while, as he glanced shoreward, he saw the glitter of an oar and a black streak that looked like a boat.

Soon a boat did come to the ice floe and Dr. Grenfell was lifted into it. He was told by his rescuers that some men on a headland cutting up seals noticed what looked like a man lying on the ice field. One of the men ran back to a village to bring someone who owned a spy glass. With this they could see that it really was a human being out on the ice which was floating out to sea. At once they manned a boat and rowed out to where the doctor lay. He was so dreadfully frostbitten by the time he was brought ashore that he could not walk and had to be dragged over the ground, like a log, to the nearest cabin. Only a man with his iron physique could have survived that experience. But to him it was all in a day's work, and as soon as he could stand up again he was back in the service. And it should be remembered that the incident of being adrift on an ice floe was only one of many narrow escapes.

Stirred by this man's devotion and heroism, and by his description of the needs of the fisherfolk along these coasts, many eagerly contributed to the mission. Lord Strathcona made the gift of a small steamer for use along the coast, and followed this by a second one, perfectly equipped for hospital service. Other contributions, large and small, came from all classes of people in Britain, Canada and the United States. The Grenfell mission branched out to furnishing milk for babies, education for boys and girls, and every other help that these people needed. The doctor lectured so often in America that his work actually became better known here than in his native land, and Americans gave generously. In time American college students and older boys from prep schools were accepted by Dr. Grenfell as volunteer workers during the summer season. These young people came to work, paying their own expenses. And Dr. Grenfell was strict; he had no use for anyone who came just for the adventure. Every volunteer had to be a real worker and take orders without question.

If any young physician had been ordered out to the Labrador Mission for a term of three years, he would have felt badly treated. But Dr. Grenfell, of his own devotion as a humanitarian, served in that difficult field not three, but forty-three years. Let us note a few of his practical achievements. He began

Sir Wilfred Thomason Grenfell

with a small coasting vessel fitted up as a hospital. By the time he had ended his service, he had established six hospitals on shore, four hospital ships, seven nursing stations, four boarding schools, fourteen industrial centers, twelve clothing distribution centers, a co-operative lumber mill, and an orphanage for children whose fathers had been lost at sea. In addition, he set up in St. Johns the King George Seamen's Institute to care for the men of the fishing fleets. Every one of these achievements may be credited to this heroic and devoted man.

Naturally, the admiration aroused by his life work brought him many honors. In 1927, King George conferred on him the order of knighthood, and he became Sir Wilfred Grenfell. Meanwhile, his story would not be complete without at least a mention of his wife. In the fall of 1908, he returned to England to fetch his mother to America. The two came back in the spring on the *Mauretania*. On the second day out he met an American girl, a fellow passenger. It was a case of love at first sight, common in story books but rare in real life. The crossing to New York took only four and a half days, but before the ship docked they were engaged. And the following autumn they were married.

After a brief honeymoon, the Grenfells sailed for the home he had made for himself at St. Anthony, on the north shore of Newfoundland. The trip was made in a blizzard, but the young bride was not discouraged. It was in that far-off spot that the three Grenfell children were born. Sir Wilfred said in one of his books that he could never have stood up to his work "but for her."

There was one interruption to the Labrador Mission that should be mentioned. When World War I broke out, Dr. Grenfell was urged by Harvard to join the Harvard Medical Unit for service in France. He accepted, was given the rank of major, and rendered invaluable service. When no longer needed for war work, he was back in Labrador, for he had many years of usefulness ahead of him.

At last, however, in 1935, the Labrador doctor's rugged constitution gave way. He realized that he could not stand the strain of the work any longer. He and Lady Grenfell then retired to their Vermont home on the shore of Lake Champlain. But he still insisted on making yearly visits to the Labrador

Mission, to see that all was going well. In 1938 his wife died, and two years later he followed her.

It is hard to make a worthy estimate of Wilfred Grenfell's life. He never forgot that meeting in a tent where he found his inspiration as a young medical student. He heard at that time, as he expressed it at the close of his life, "a vital call . . . for things that I could do in the world." How well he answered that call can better be felt than expressed in words. King George gave him the title of knight. Long before that he had demonstrated his peculiar right to recognition as a shining knight who gave his whole life to slaying the dragons of misery, starvation and pain that were torturing the fisherfolk of the Labrador and Newfoundland coasts.

ALBERT SCHWEITZER

ALBERT SCHWEITZER

XIII. ALBERT SCHWEITZER

January 14, 1875—

THE SUBJECT OF this final chapter, Albert Schweitzer, is, like Helen Keller, still living and active in the work which made them both famous as humanitarians. It is pleasant to know that our generation also can boast of these two individuals who carry on the bright torch of human kindliness handed down by the saintly men and women of earlier days.

Albert Schweitzer was the son of a village pastor living in the province of Alsace. He was born only four years after the Franco-Prussian War, when that province, together with its neighbor, Lorraine, was taken from France by Germany as a prize of victory. World War I gave it back to France. This changing back-and-forth as a borderland between the two nations has resulted in the Alsatians being at home in two languages, French and German. That is true of Albert Schweitzer, who has, all through his career, written and lectured in either tongue with equal ease.

As a baby, Albert was so sickly that his parents feared he never would live to grow up, but evidently the fine country air among the hills did more than the doctors, for he grew big and rugged as a lad. Later, as a man, his constitution was tough enough to withstand the worst climate in the world for a white man, that part of Africa where he founded his famous medical mission.

The boy's earliest interest was music. His father played the piano at home, and at church young Albert was fascinated by the organ. This passion for music he never lost. Even in the jungles of Africa he played for relaxation on a specially built piano presented to him by friends when he first set out on his mission.

Famous Humanitarians

Oddly enough, when one thinks of the rich scholarship of Albert Schweitzer in his manhood years, his school record was not good; his teacher reported him as slow and inattentive. But in those days teaching was more a matter of whipping than of interesting the pupil. He had the usual rough and tumble life of the playground, and he found out to his satisfaction that he could out-wrestle the biggest boy in the school. The only thing that really worried him was the fact that, as the pastor's son, he was better dressed than the others, and he told his father that he wanted to have the same kind of clothes the other village boys wore.

One event of those school years is worth noting. His friends invited him one day to go hunting with them. He had his slingshot and had always been good at hitting a target. As they went out into the country, they came upon a tree, the top of which was alive with birds.

"Hey, get that big fellow!" cried a boy. But just then the church bells clanged and at the sound all the birds flew away. "The music," wrote Albert Schweitzer in later years, "drove the commandment into my heart, 'Thou shalt not kill!' It was one of the great experiences of my childhood and youth." A hatred of killing formed in the boy's mind then and there. It was not only the killing for fun, but any killing that was not really necessary. That feeling was strong in him as a grown man, and he called it "a reverence for life."

Another incident about this time also made an unforgettable impression on Albert's character. There was an old Jewish trader who used to pass through the village with his donkey cart. The boys used to jeer at him and tug at his coat. When Albert was with them one day and saw and heard what they were doing, he was surprised to see the old man turn around and, in-stead of cursing his tormenters, he smiled at them as much as to say, "I know what boys are like; I was once one myself." That kindly smile was too much for Albert. On the peddler's next visit the boy went up to him, shook his hand, and then walked alongside the donkey cart, talking as if the old man were a member of his own family. If the other boys were surprised, they knew better than to poke fun at Albert because he could out-fight any one of them.

So, in one way and another, the boy's character was forming all the time that he was working over his school books and his piano lessons. From the piano he went to the organ, the instrument he was destined to know more about than anyone else in the world. In fact, his progress was so rapid that, while only a teen-age lad, his teacher, the organist at St. Stephen's church, allowed him to take over one Sunday morning for the full service, and before a congregation that packed the church. It was this same teacher who introduced Albert to the works of the great composers of organ music, notably Johann Sebastian Bach. Years later, Albert Schweitzer wrote a two-volume work on Bach, which is still the last word on that composer.

For his university work, young Schweitzer went to Strasbourg, the capital of Alsace. By a strange chance the room that he rented, in what was called the Old Fish Market, happened to be the same one which the German poet Goethe had occupied as a student more than a hundred years before. Perhaps that fact helped to give Albert Schweitzer a special interest in that outstanding genius, because in the years to come, he became the world's foremost authority on Goethe.

Like every other youth in Germany, Albert had to serve his year of military service. In spite of the hard routine of the barracks, he used to study at night when all his comrades were asleep. Strange to say, in this atmosphere his interest began to turn to religion, and he decided to take a degree in that subject. He felt the need of a real purpose in life, and came to the decision that, after a few more years of study, especially in music, he would put all behind him and go to some "dark area" of the world where he could devote all the rest of his life to serving people who were in desperate need. Meanwhile, he began work on a life of Christ which attracted world-wide attention. In connection with his music he conducted a campaign to save the old, hand-made organs in the churches, which he discovered were so much better in tone than the new factory-made ones.

He was only twenty-four when he not only had his degree in theology but also was appointed pastor of a church in Strasbourg. In this charge he was successful from the first; the only complaint the congregation had to offer was an unusual one, that Pastor Schweitzer's sermons were too short! Next, while still in his twenties, he was appointed head of a theological seminary. And all the while he was being called on, the length and breadth of Europe, for organ recitals, for he had no equal on that instrument. Every one who knew him predicted for him a dazzling career.

Then one day he read a pamphlet issued by a missionary society in Paris which described the desperate need for missionaries and doctors in French Equatorial Africa. "My search is over," said he to himself, "this is my mission in life." But he knew that for such work a medical education was essential. To the astonishment of his friends, he went back to the University of Strasbourg to study medicine.

When he explained that he was determined to devote his life to the natives of darkest Africa, there was a great outcry of protest. "You are throwing away your life, your many-sided genius. You are casting your pearls before swine. Those natives are hardly better than animals." But he was unshaken, and by 1911 he had won his doctor's degree in medicine. From the medical school at Strasbourg he went to Paris, taking special courses in tropical diseases.

Meanwhile, he had met Helene Breslau, daughter of a Jewish professor in the University, and they had fallen in love. He told her of his plan, but added sadly that it would be too full of danger and hardship for her, because the region he had picked out for his mission was, as he said, "the most unhealthy spot on earth."

"I will take a training course in nursing," she replied calmly, "and then you won't be able to get along without me."

And so they were married, in 1912, and together they prepared for the mission. One big problem was to raise money for medical supplies, but friends started them off with a gift of $5,000 for the purpose. On Good Friday, 1913, Dr. Schweitzer and his wife boarded the train en route to their "dark area."

When they landed on the coast of French Africa, and as they went inland, everything they saw was depressing and discouraging. They went up a river in a steamboat and then had to continue the journey in a native dugout. The living quarters provided for them in advance was a small house. The one pleasant touch about it was the fact that the native children had decorated it in advance with flowers and palm leaves. Worn out by their journey, the Schweitzers went to bed, but that first night their rooms were filled with flying cockroaches; spiders and ants crawled everywhere; hungry mosquitoes poured in at the windows; and in the distance there was the steady throb of native drums. By the time they had caught a few winks of sleep they were awakened by a group of well-meaning native children singing a hymn that a missionary had taught them.

The story of the heroic battle that Dr. and Mrs. Schweitzer carried on to establish a medical mission at the edge of the primeval forest is a long one and only a few events can be touched on in this brief sketch. The doctor's "reverence for life" was given a hard test from the first day, when he found insect pests, vermin, and rats besieging the house, and outdoors wild animals and poisonous snakes that everywhere threatened human life.

He wanted to build a hospital at once, but discovered that he couldn't get any labor because all the men were busy at a lumber camp. But the sick natives came pouring in, begging to be treated, many in very bad condition. The first hospital had to be a shack which had been used as a chicken house. This, cleaned and whitewashed, accommodated the first desperate cases. For his operating table, the doctor used a folding cot lent him by a religious mission near by. Then calls came for cases that could not be moved and meant expeditions in native dugouts upriver. It can easily be imagined that Dr. Schweitzer had work enough for a hundred doctors. At first he had to do it all, helped only by his noble wife. And, just to make matters worse, hardly had the Schweitzers arrived when word was brought to them that a tribe of fierce cannibals had moved into the vicinity!

Altogether, it was a "dark area" with a vengeance. The natives themselves were as backward and as degraded peoples as could be found anywhere in the world. Not only did they live in terror of the witch doctors, but they used poisons as a convenient way to get rid of personal enemies.

As soon as he could get labor, Dr. Schweitzer began the building of his hospital; but before the end of their first year in the jungle, both he and his wife were laid low with tropical anemia and had to be taken to the coast for treatment and change of climate.

Soon came news of a great war in Europe. The Schweitzers were devoting their lives to serve the natives of French Equatorial Africa, but because they came from Alsace they were enemy aliens to the French government. Armed native soldiers arrived who arrested them and forbade them even to speak to either whites or natives. This idiotic order forced the closing of the hospital and the end of the mission service. In September, 1917, these two devoted people were brought back to France as prisoners and sent to an internment camp in the Pyrenees mountains. That camp had in ancient days been a big monastery, and what heating system there was in that building can easily be imagined. A severe winter followed, causing much suffering. Evidently it never occurred to the French officials that these civilian men and women of all ages might need a doctor. It happened that Albert Schweitzer was the only physician in the concentration camp, and he was kept busy playing the Good Samaritan, although both he and his wife, after five years in African heat, suffered greatly from the cold and were none too well themselves.

After a while they were transferred to a camp for Alsatians only, and then they were exchanged and sent home through Switzerland. At once, the Mayor of Strasbourg begged Dr. Schweitzer to serve as physician in the city hospital, and he gladly accepted, at the same time serving again as pastor of his former church.

Thereafter, when the war was over, he wrote and lectured on behalf of his African medical mission, but it was not until 1924 that he was able to return to the scene of his labors. This time his wife was unable to go with him, because of a breakdown of her own health. On his arrival he found everything in ruins. Every building that he had put up had collapsed in his absence, except a small hut of corrugated iron. He had to begin all over again from the ground up, but he did just that. Nothing could discourage this man. By the fall of 1925 he had rebuilt his hospital, and brought in two doctors and two nurses from Europe. Yet hardly was the new hospital finished when a terrible famine and an epidemic of dysentery made it necessary to move the whole plant two miles farther up the river to a larger site.

The rest of the story must be reduced to a few words. It was always, through the years, the same self-sacrificing devotion to the savages for whom no one else had seemed to care. He would repeatedly return to Europe to raise money by lecture tours. In 1939 he turned to America for help as well, and received

Albert Schweitzer

a generous response. In that very year, World War II broke out, and though he was no longer an enemy alien to the French government, that war made it very hard to get needed supplies.

Ten years later, in 1949, he made his first visit to the United States, on the invitation of the University of Chicago, to be the principal speaker at a Goethe celebration, with the promise of a fee of two million francs for his hospital. And in California an Albert Schweitzer Fellowship was organized to help keep his mission going financially.

Meanwhile many honors came to him from universities in Europe and America. It was an American who wrote these words of him in a leading religious magazine:

"We, too, recognize him as the greatest living man, the only person ever to earn doctorates in philosophy, theology, medicine and music, and the world's foremost missionary." The same writer also described him as "the simplest and most human of men." It is all true, but the last statement would have pleased him best. Because, for all his saintliness and intellectual achievements, he never took himself seriously, never lost his sense of humor. Once the chairman at one of his lectures asked him how he would like to be introduced.

"Just say," was the answer, "this fellow who looks like a Scottish collie is Albert Schweitzer." That was in laughing allusion to the fact that his bushy hair would never stay brushed.

And once, after a specially hard day of interviews on his American visit, one more reporter bustled up to the great man, with pencil and pad ready. "Please, Dr. Schweitzer, will you give me a statement on your reverence for life?"

"Oh, I believe in it," was the smiling reply, "and I want you to have some, too, a reverence just now for my life. I am very tired."

As to his modesty, these words as spoken to another American, Fulton Oursler, are typical: "You may think it is a wonderful life my wife and I have in the equatorial jungle. That is merely where we happen to be. But you can have a still more wonderful life by staying where you happen to be and putting your soul to the test in a thousand little trials and winning triumphs of love . . . It calls for strength of will and the determination to love, the greatest test of a man. But in this hard 'second job' is to be found the only true happiness."

In his own words, Dr. Schweitzer passes off those forty years of the hardest kind of service in Africa as "merely where we happen to be." Anyone else can have "a still more wonderful life by staying where you happen to be," and living the life of unselfish service. Like all other truly great souls, Dr. Schweitzer's outstanding characteristic is his humility. To this generation, torn by wars and the threat of wars, his life is a shining inspiration for human brotherhood.

INDEX